Marketing With A Heart

How To Use Trust Based Marketing For Greater Income, Influence, and Impact

Ben Gioia

Marketing With A Heart
How To Use Trust Based Marketing For Greater Income, Influence, and Impact

"Before you start reading...I have a gift for you."

Visit **marketingwithaheart.com/bookgift**

It's my thanks to you...for reading this book and because I know you want to help people live happier, more productive, peaceful lives.

What you learn by reading *Marketing With A Heart* will help you...whether you're an executive, entrepreneur, small business owner, speaker, author, coach, consultant, or other purpose driven leader.

You will become an excellent communicator, a better marketer (even if you don't consider yourself a marketer), and a better leader. AND there's more...

Your gift is the Marketing With A Heart Quickstart Kickstart AND The 10X+ Content Multiplier.

It's a fast, fun, FREE training (valued at $97) + framework (valued at $47) that will help you:

1) be more productive; strategic, and efficient;

2) position yourself as a leader, expert, or authority and maximize your exposure;

3) locate and develop relationships with the best clients or customers for your business;

4) deliver a ton of value that will transform their lives and have them raving about you;

5) communicate effectively, so they take action that's right for them and right for you.

What you learn will get people to your website, onto your list, calling you for a consultation, investing in your products and services, and telling the world about what you offer...because it's changing their lives for the better.

What People Are Saying
About Ben Gioia and His Strategies

"Ben is a coach, author, speaker, and seminar leader who truly cares about making a positive difference in the lives of others. In addition, he is a very smart businessperson who can tremendously help you grow your business by sharing his Marketing With A Heart™ philosophy. It is my sincere honor to introduce you to Ben and his brilliant book: Marketing With A Heart!*"*

—James Malinchak
Featured on the ABC Hit TV Show, *"Secret Millionaire"*
The World's #1 Speaker Trainer
Founder, BigMoneySpeaker.com

"Coaches, consultants, teachers, and others with a message of service: read this book so you can truly see that it's not only possible, but of greater value—to have your marketing and promotions be as high in ethics, integrity, and service as your core product or service. Join me in following Ben's lead. Together we can elevate and enlighten the practice of reaching out and offering our gifts and talents to those whom we are meant to serve."

—Lou D'Alo
Founder of PowerUpCoaching.com
Marketing for Enlightened Business Owners

"This is a must read for any salesperson, business owner or entrepreneur. Marketing With A Heart *is not just about marketing and selling. It is about communicating with people. Ben shares his incredible heart felt experiences and principles to help build lasting relationships in any business. I am recommending this book to all of my clients."*

—John Formica
The "Ex-Disney Guy"
America's Customer Experience Coach, Speaker and Author

"What resonates the most with me about Ben is his heartfelt and patient approach, blended with skillful coaching aimed at achieving results. Ben offers an array of ideas, resources and a strategic plan that gives traction to your vision while staying connected to the heart of your business."

—Annette Segal
CEO and Founder, The Valiant Group
Leadership Coaching For Executives and Consultants

"I have known Ben Gioia for quite some time. He is genuine, insightful, and very capable. His approach to marketing in Marketing With a Heart *is refreshing, effective and a breath of fresh air for those tired of the 'All for Me' and 'Buyer Beware' style of business that seems to rule the world. A must read for anyone doing business in this digital decade."*

—Kellan Fluckiger, The Execution Mentor
Speaker, Author, Creator of "Break The Cage"
BreakTheCageNow.com

"I have never been one to really care much about marketing and branding, and honestly, I've always thought of people who do as the "enemy" to what I'm about. After talking with Ben for an hour, he actually got me excited about branding and packaging my ideas, and that's quite a feat!"

—Kathleen Keller, PhD
Mark T. Greenberg Professor for the
Study of Children's Health & Development
Assistant Professor, Depts. of Nutritional Sciences and
Food Science at The Pennsylvania State University

*"*Marketing With A Heart *is a key addition to your favorite books as it will make immediate and powerful changes in every aspect of the way you communicate and operate your business...and your life. It's a motivational read that inspires and Ben Gioia shifts your thinking and proves that you can truly make money while making a*

difference. Even better, the more money you make, the more people you can serve."

—Tracy Repchuk
International Bestselling Author & World Renowned Speaker
Get Instant Online Impact With A Fully Branded
End To End Website Presence in Under 60 Days

"Ben Gioia brings "the heart"! His undeniable methods of successful, heart-felt marketing, easily make him a one-percenter in his field of expertise. He offers THE TRUTH—zero fluff...zero BS! To put it straight—Ben walks-the-walk! If you desire battle-tested results and are literally chomping at the bit to reach the summit of success, then stop wasting time, get off your ass and buy Ben's book...NOW!

—Chris Warner
Author of *Master Your Confidence*
Actor/Speaker/The Blacksmith of Badass
Forging the Young Men of Today Into
Strong, Respected Leaders of Tomorrow

"Who can you trust? Hard to tell. Read this book."

—Brad Blanton
Author of *Radical Honesty:
How To Transform Your Life By Telling The Truth*
RadicalHonesty.com

"Reading Ben's book is a reminder of what happens when business follows the heart—we call that doing the right thing. Clarity, focus, gratitude, and purpose will come with the guidance from this book!"

—Jeff Marcous
Chief Evolutionary Office, Dharma Merchant Services
The first payment processing company to integrate
and profit from Conscious Capitalism.

"The principles of Marketing With A Heart are not just for marketing. They can be applied to sales, networking, running your business, and yes...even your personal life. They're based on

timeless principles of life. It's all about communicating with authenticity and integrity while striving for the best possible outcome...for everyone involved. Thank you, Ben!"

—LaVonna Roth
Author, Speaker & Consultant
Minds That Matter, Inc.

"The road less taken can often be the smartest, especially long term, if it leads to win-win. Almost anyone can do a one shot sale. It takes a leader to make it sustainable. Thanks to you, Ben, for your valuable insights. This is a great book for everyone who wants to build relationships that last and a profitable, sustainable, competitive business in the process."

—George H. Schofield, PhD
Speaker, Author of *After 50 It's Up To Us*
Expert on High Quality Life After 50
GeorgeSchofield.com

"'Marketing with a Heart' *is what resonated initially. The name tells me about you as an individual and how you approach marketing, the type of projects you work on, etc. Your background with nonprofits was important as many of my clients are nonprofits. Your calm, quiet, gentle manner is very helpful. Some marketing folks are all hype, excess energy and "blare." Your calm demeanor is greatly appreciated.*"

—Judy Whalen
Founder & CEO
CenterForStrategicChange.com
ShopliftingIsStealing.com

"Starting a new business or project is hard, at any age, but it was especially daunting for me, because I had worked for corporations for 30+ years. Going out of my comfort zone meant taking risks, and it was great to have Ben to bounce ideas off of because friends and family are not objective. Ben gave me useful tools and ways to think about what services I had to offer and how I could position my services/businesses in a marketable way."

—Ann Powell
Founder and Director
Responsive Edit

"I've been working with Ben for over two years now and he is fantastic marketing consultant. He provides high quality, well thought through strategies and campaigns. A high level of customer service and integrity is also a strong asset of Ben's work. I would recommend Ben to anyone looking for an honest, reliable marketing professional to work with their team and help get them results."

—Sara Nguyen
President and Founder
SocialMediaRocketeer.com

"Ben is a great coach who brings many skills, a depth of knowledge and understanding of marketing and heartfelt joy to his work. After a session with Ben I feel like my compass settings have been recalibrated to True North."

—Jerry Rosser, LMFT
President and Founder
PsychologyofJoy.com

"Ben taught me to marshall my time and resources effectively, challenged me to find my value (something we coaches tend to do: undervalue), and assisted me increase my monthly fee by 40% (the largest limit to that percentage being my fears, something he can't control). Ben's an honest down-to-earth guy who knows his stuff. I strongly recommend him!"

—Kenji Oshima
Business Coach For Ultra Successful Entrepreneurs
CoachKenji.com

Table of Contents

Marketing is how you can change lives with your message. This is why the right kind of marketing is critical to your success. You'll discover perspectives and approaches to high integrity marketing, selling, and influence that are simple, powerful, and you can use right now.

Chapter 2 (Purpose)   59

It's the "why" that fuels your passion and your mission. It's the strategy for making your dreams into reality. It's how you balance your long-term vision with day-to-day action so you can inspire, persuade, and transform lives.

Chapter 3 (Profit)   87

While your message will change one life, your marketing can change thousands, if not millions of lives. You'll learn simple principles to communicate more persuasively, make more money, help more people, and inspire others through your message, work, and example.

Chapter 4 (Principles)   113

Principles are the foundation of Marketing With A Heart™ and are the bedrock for People, Purpose, and Profit. You'll discover perspectives and insights about your journey to success, service, being happy, and creating the business and life you want. You'll also learn what makes a business truly sustainable, more profitable, and impactful.

A Note To You, The Reader

No matter where you are in business—succeeding beyond your wildest dreams, building toward your next leap, or starting something new—I know that you and I have something in common.

We want to help people live happier, more productive, peaceful lives.

As a speaker, author, consultant, and coach, I will help you tell your story and deliver your message (in the right language and to the right audience) so it creates greater income, influence, and impact in the world.

As a dedicated student of marketing, conscious leadership, human potential, and the spiritual path, I can say with absolute certainty that Marketing With A Heart™ is the most practical, proven approach to marketing, selling, and service.

It's a philosophy of business success, personal happiness, and reaching your highest potential while helping people.

The principles of Marketing With A Heart™ have already helped thousands of people…and they can absolutely help you, your business, and the people you serve.

I'm honored to share this with you and am grateful for your time, energy, and attention.

I've done everything I can to make sure this book creates a powerful transformation in your business and your life.

This book is like nothing you've read before.

Get ready. And thank you for sharing this journey with me.

Cheers,

Ben

People, Purpose, and Profit: Conscious Marketing and Conscious Business Will Boost Your Bottom Line

It's not just a trend...it's a cultural shift that's redefining business in the 21st century. It's how to become more profitable, more successful, and more sustainable. It's also the right thing to do. Because conscious business is more fun and fulfilling than just chasing after profit...at the expense of your health, your relationships, your happiness, and the planet.

It's what companies like Ben & Jerry's, Google, IBM, Starbuck's, Trader Joe's, Method, Patagonia, Zappos, General Mills, and Whole Foods are putting into practice every day.

It's what thought leaders like Accenture, Goldman Sachs, Harvard Business School, McKinsey and Company, and PricewaterhouseCoopers are proving time and again.

It's happening in my business. It's happening for my clients.

Conscious business outperforms traditional business. And it's not just a handful of organizations or results. The Dow Jones Sustainability Index has performed an average of 36.1% better than the traditional Dow Jones Index over a period of five years.

In addition, conscious marketing MASSIVELY outperforms traditional marketing. Studies show that you'll invest only 10-25% of what everybody else in your industry is spending on their marketing. This happens when you create authentic relationships with your clients, customers, and other stakeholders—while giving them tremendous value—so they literally become the voice of your business.

People will sing your praises, give you tons of free exposure, and bring a flood of new and repeat business to your door.

Are you ready?

About Ben

Ben Gioia ("joy-a") is the premier speaker, author, coach, and authority on conscious marketing, selling, and service—key elements for business success in the 21st century. He is the President and Founder of Marketing With A Heart™.

According to Ben, service is the core of the best marketing, selling, and leadership...especially when you can help people be happier, more successful, and more fulfilled.

Marketing With a Heart™ is a system, strategy, and philosophy based on authentic communication, high integrity, conscious leadership, and service. Marketing With a Heart™ puts an end to manipulative marketing, sleazy selling, and profits that come at the expense of people and the planet. It offers a new bottom line for business—people, purpose, AND profit—which creates sustainable, proven, long-term success and fulfillment.

Ben wrote the #1 best seller *Marketing With A Heart: How To Use Trust Based Marketing For Greater Income, Influence, And Impact*. He's also the Marketing and Communications Board Chair for Conscious Capitalism Bay Area.

His book offers revolutionary perspectives on marketing, selling, conscious leadership, communication, and running your business in alignment with your principles...so you can create a fulfilled and joyful life.

Ben delivers speeches and trainings for purpose driven leaders, associations, organizations, and companies around the country, around the world, and on the web.

Onstage and online, Ben inspires, energizes, and engages his audience.

He invites people to use the principles of Marketing With a Heart™ to create greater income, influence, and impact in the world. And to have more fun while doing it!

Before starting his own business, Ben worked with three nonprofits, seven startups, and produced three magazines (published by Hearst and Condé Nast).

He was a key member of the team that launched both *My Generation* and *AARP The Magazine* (circulation 35 million).

Before the first person was drenched and shivering from The Ice Bucket Challenge, Ben did the marketing and patient services for The ALS Association (Lou Gehrig's disease) in the San Francisco Bay Area.

He also helped with an organizational consolidation between the Bay Area and Los Angeles Chapters of the Association.

This led to greater revenue, improved patient services (covering half the state of California), and a more efficient organizational structure.

Ben weaves his amazing life story into what he teaches.

Almost dying four times in 72 hours (while traveling in India) completely changed his outlook on life and crystallized his desire to make a positive impact in the world.

When he got back to the U.S., he soon became a hospice volunteer.

Then he created and launched Marketing With A Heart™.

Ben helps people use the right language and tell their story the right way—to inspire, lead, and transform lives.

How can Ben help you? Find out today by visiting marketingwithaheart.com/services

He'd love to hear from you right now!

Welcome To Marketing With A Heart™

There are years of negative perceptions about marketing, selling, and influence: that they are everything from unpleasant…to straight up evil.

Because they've not been done consciously.

That's why I created Marketing With A Heart™.

Marketing, selling, and influence are service…when you do them with the right intention and what you're offering will help people live happier, more productive, peaceful lives.

Marketing is the true language of service.

Marketing is how you communicate with and influence people in a way that inspires them to take action…so they can be more successful, more fulfilled, and have more fun.

When you communicate with authenticity and integrity, you can inspire people to make the choices that will benefit them and benefit you.

Here's the difference between "old school" marketing and Marketing With A Heart™.

"Old school" marketing is what you do TO people: pressure, fear, manipulation, lies, false hope, sales tactics, and hard closes. (Think of the stereotypical, sleazy, used car salesman in a cheap, plaid suit.)

Marketing With A Heart™ is what you do FOR people: inspiring, educating, adding value, creating trust, developing relationships, and changing lives. It's a win-win.

Marketing With A Heart™ is a revolutionary philosophy and successful business strategy because it provides a personal approach to making money while making a difference.

By learning and applying these simple principles and strategies, you'll be able to make your business more profitable and successful. This comes from cultivating trust, building relationships, and inviting your audience to take action because you understand what they care about, are speaking to them in their language, and are delivering value.

(You've discovered their story and shared yours with them.)

You'll also attract the right people to form partnerships and strategic alliances so you can make an even greater positive impact in the world.

* * *

There's one more important thing that I want you to know.

I couldn't have created Marketing With A Heart™ by myself.

After you read the book, I invite you to check out the Acknowledgments. If you just take a moment to read the names, you'll help me honor the people who've contributed to my success. You may even know somebody.

I want to offer an extra special thanks to my coach and friend Lou D'Alo. It is said that if you want to be successful, hang out with successful people and do what they do.

I hang out with Lou as much as possible…whether it's on a call, at a live event, or just listening to recordings of his coaching and trainings.

He is a Personal and Business Success Coach for Enlightened Entrepreneurs. Yeah!

I am grateful and honored to have such a person, a friend, and a master to emulate.

Because he is doing and being so much of what I want to do and who I want to be.

Thanks Lou!

Why You're Here

You're a visionary, a leader, whether you're helping one person or changing the lives of millions. You're here for a reason...and reading these words right now.

You have a story, message, product, or service that you need to get out there.

And you need to make the money that will support your mission, your business, and your life.

I wrote this for you. People need what you've got RIGHT NOW. There has never been a more pivotal time in history.

As someone who wants to help people, it's imperative that you know enough about marketing to effectively communicate with and influence your audience—as well as provide leadership, inspiration, and guidance to the multiple people who will support you and your mission.

And not just any old marketing...conscious marketing.

Wherever you are right now is both temporary and exactly where you're supposed to be.

You've arrived at this moment to learn what you must learn, so you can continue to become the person you need to be, and the person that the world needs.

This will help you create the life you truly want and make more money...so you can succeed in business and serve more people.

And since you're reading this, I know that you want to help people live happier, more productive, peaceful lives. Me too.

I'm here to help you use the right language and deliver your message the right way—to inspire, influence, and transform lives.

How To Use This Book

Most businesses still (unfortunately) focus on an antiquated, unsustainable bottom line: profit.

That's a losing battle that's doomed to failure...and is the cause of numerous problems around the world.

Marketing With A Heart™ redefines the bottom line: **People, Purpose, and Profit**...which is sustainable, profitable, and a lot more fun and fulfilling.

This is the framework for how I've written the book. In each chapter, you'll find teaching points and case studies.

I've also added a fourth section, Principles, which is the foundation for People, Purpose, and Profit. You can read this book from front to back. Or open to any page and start there.

PEOPLE

Marketing
With A Heart™

A Principle Based Approach

PURPOSE   **PROFIT**

PEOPLE

Marketing is how you can change lives with your message. Whether you're an entrepreneur, executive, politician, speaker, author, coach, trainer, consultant, or other visionary who's committed to making positive change in the world....you are a leader. Conscious leadership is about shaping the future. And conscious marketing is the tool that makes it happen.

When you're promoting, presenting, partnering, or producing, sooner or later you'll need to align people with your vision and then inspire them to take action. This is why the right kind of marketing is critical. Marketing With A Heart™ will make your prospects buy and your stakeholders buy in. You'll discover perspectives and approaches to high integrity marketing, selling, influence, and leadership that you can use right away.

PURPOSE

Purpose is the "why" that fuels your passion and your mission. It's the strategy for making your dreams into reality. It's how you balance your long-term vision with day-to-day action. It's knowing what guides you from within...which helps you make the right decisions, even the hard ones.

When you know your Purpose, your work is more fun and fulfilling and an expression of who you are. You get more of the right things done faster and with much less stress. This supports your mission and your ability to transform people's lives. It's a win-win for everyone your business and life touches.

PROFIT

While your message will change one life, your marketing can change thousands, if not millions of lives, when done the right way. Marketing With A Heart™ gives you the tools for greater income, influence, and impact...that are easy and that you can use right now. It begins by getting to know your audience and speaking to them, in their language, about the things that are most important to them.

Whether you're online, onstage, or the next presenter on the agenda, you'll learn simple principles and strategies that will help you communicate more persuasively, be more profitable, help more people, and inspire others through your message, work, and example.

PRINCIPLES

Principles are the foundation of Marketing With A Heart™ and are the bedrock for People, Purpose, and Profit. You'll discover perspectives and insights about your journey to success, service, being happy, and creating the business and life you want. You'll also learn what makes a business truly sustainable (and therefore more profitable and impactful).

Actually, why wait? Let me tell you right now.

It's the choices you make. Your choices impact everyone (inside and outside of the workplace)...as well as the environment, your partners, other stakeholders, and the public.

What you choose to think, say, and do will affect you, everyone around you, and every person who is alive today...then down to the great grandchildren—of your children's—great grandchildren. So you can choose profit at the expense of everything and everyone else. Or you choose to serve others, do business with integrity, influence with compassion, lead with empathy, and take personal responsibility...to create the business and life that you want.

My Story:
From Mess To Success and I'm Grateful To Be Alive

Marketing With A Heart™ was born from the journey of my life: careers, day-to-day living, and by traveling around the country and around the world.

Let's step back a few years: three nonprofits, five publications, seven startups, and 16 countries....

•Before Marketing With A Heart™, I produced three magazines (published by Hearst and Condé Nast).

•I was part of the team that launched both *My Generation* and *AARP The Magazine* (circulation 35 million).

•I also did the marketing for The ALS Association (a few years before the popular ALS Ice Bucket Challenge.)

Along the way, I ran into a wall. One day I woke up and realized that my life looked good on paper but nothing felt good on the inside. The drugs and parties didn't help, although they were fun for a little while...

But, I was basically taking the express elevator to rock bottom. I had to do something. So I traveled to South Africa. I witnessed the devastating effects of apartheid and racism. I traveled to India and listened to horrific stories of cultural genocide and torture from Tibetan refugees.

Even after all this, I started realizing that no matter what was happening in my experience, I was in charge of my response. Therefore, I was in charge of my happiness...and my life. Period.

In India, my life changed, radically. While trekking in the mountains, I almost died (more than once) in 72 hours.

Here's what happened.

My bus barely made the turn while going up a mountain (the rear destroyed the guardrail and swung out over the abyss). At the beginning of a two day trek, I ran from a massive forest fire. The next day I stumbled upon a poisonous snake and then later, a mountain lion (who was, thankfully, more scared than me.)

Finally, while riding in a jeep down a winding mountain road (no guardrails this time), the driver chose to save gas by shutting off the engine and coasting. (The whole time, we were passing buses, trucks, and horse drawn carts. We had 16 people inside and on the roof of a jeep that only seated eight.)

The driver spent the entire ride in deep, animated conversation with two people up front. He drove with one hand while constantly changing the cassette with the other. He never found the right music.

Somehow, I made it to the bottom of the mountain. Later, I made it home...with so much gratitude for this gift of life...and a fire inside to create massive positive impact. (And to do it as soon as possible, because I didn't know if I'd be alive for 60 more years or 60 more minutes.)

One of the first things I did was to become a hospice volunteer.

I realized that I wanted to help people. And I knew that I could exponentially impact more people by inspiring, influencing, and supporting the individuals and businesses who are committed to creating positive change.

At the same time, I began to see entrepreneurs and organizations using business as a force for good: Craig Newmark, Tony Hawk, Oprah Winfrey, Whole Foods, Zappos, Method, TOMS Shoes, and Ben & Jerry's, just to name a few.

So a few years later, I created Marketing With A Heart™.

The Philosophy of Marketing With A Heart™

Marketing, selling, and leadership are service, when you align your vision with people's dreams—and inspire them to take action—so it's a win-win for everyone.

There are four things that I know to be true: 1.) We all want to be happy, healthy, safe, and secure. 2.) We all create our experience (based on our habits, conditioning, beliefs, and attitudes). 3.) There is no actual, tangible, physical separation between you and me (on an atomic or on a spiritual level). 4.) Therefore...what I think, say, do, and choose directly and immediately affects me and affects you... and ultimately everyone else.

So Marketing With A Heart™ is about connection and understanding through stories. When you tell your stories, people will feel empathy toward you. When you discover their stories, you feel empathy toward them. All of a sudden this empathy becomes Synergetic Empathy™...it's now a two way street. You understand them, they understand you, and you have everything you need for effective marketing, conscious communication, and authentic human connection.

Marketing With A Heart™ is about nourishing yourself with positive thoughts, words, choices, and actions...plus the right knowledge and skills so you can succeed.

Marketing With A Heart™ is about serving others, doing business with integrity, influencing with compassion, leading with empathy, and taking responsibility for your choices...so you can create the business and life that you want.

Why A Principle Based Approach To
Marketing, Selling, and Service?

In *The 7 Habits of Highly Effective People,* Stephen Covey states that there are only three constants in life: change, choice, and principles.

Marketing With A Heart™ is a principle based approach to marketing, selling, and service.

Why principles?

Because principles are like gravity. They are constant and reliable.

They stay the same regardless of time, who you're with, or where you are (assuming you're not in outer space).

Principles are not the same as values. Here's why.

• Values change according to time, place, situations, and the people involved. ("A woman's place is in the home" is a powerful example. Thankfully we've come a long way from that, at least in some parts of the world.)

• Values create your beliefs: how you see the world, how you relate to other people, how you interpret your experiences, and how you choose to act. (And sometimes you may not even understand why you do what you do.)

• Values and beliefs affect your life, business, marketing, selling, leadership, and communication.

And some of your values and beliefs may not be supporting your success.

Why?

Because values and beliefs come from many people and places outside of ourselves.

These include families, friends, cultures, schools, religions, societies, media, direct experience, and the workplace.

Do any of these sound familiar?

"Well, that's just the way life is."

"Profit is the most important thing in any business."

"You can't do business and do good."

All of us have values and beliefs that we never chose for ourselves, but somehow they became a part of us. And part of the business world.

And that's a big problem.

Because most businesses have only one value that's the driving force behind everything they do: profit.

Now, profit is critical to business success.

Don't get me wrong.

But profit as a value—by itself—is unsustainable for everyone involved (the customers, the business, partners, stakeholders, and affiliates), for the environment, for long term success, and for your happiness and fulfillment.

Because when you win, someone else has to lose.

That's why Marketing With A Heart™ takes a principle based approach instead. It's an approach based on truth respect, integrity, service, gratitude, responsibility, and love.

Win-win.

The 7 Principles of Marketing With Heart™

1. Principle of High Integrity Success

I measure success through the people I serve, how I am living and expressing my purpose (in my life and business), and the value I create.

Since negative thoughts, words, and actions yield negative results, I do my best to focus on the positive, even in the most challenging circumstances.

Sometimes this requires changing my habits, beliefs, perspectives, and attitudes because they affect others, and me.

2. Principle of The Other Person's Shoes

All of my choices need to be informed by more than just my own perspective. When I am about to make a choice, I remind myself to ask these questions.

- How will this choice affect my client?
- What about other people that my business touches?
- The environment?
- The community?
- The people who are alive, seven generations down the line from right now?
- Will everyone win based on the choice that I am about to make?

3. Principle of Truth and Respect

What I think, say, and do affects me and the people around me. Because of this, I do my best to be aware of my thoughts words, and actions.

- Do I feel open and calm, or constricted and defensive?

- Am I telling the truth?
- Am I treating people with respect?
- How am I standing?
- What is my tone of voice?
- How can I serve others while making my business profitable and successful?

4. Principle of Growing and Sharing Wealth

I am in business to make a difference and create wealth. The more money I make, the more people I can help.

Am I creating wealth responsibly, using it to serve others, and taking care of myself and my relationships...as I take this journey?

I know money is a result of my service and the value I bring to others, not the goal unto itself.

5. Principle of Community

I do my best to focus on cooperation. I know I have a far greater reach and impact by working with clients, partners, and others who, in turn, will reach out and positively affect others.

The only competition is with myself. Therefore, I strive to grow and achieve more each day so I can become more profitable, help more people, and inspire others through my message, work, and example.

6. Principle of Personal Responsibility

Because all people want to be happy, healthy, safe, and secure (just like you and me), I do my best to make choices that are aligned with my principles and are an expression of who I am...while being mindful of how these choices affect others.

I recognize that every person creates their reality and experiences based on habits, conditioning, beliefs, and attitudes.

Because of this, I take full responsibility for everything that happens to me as well as how I affect other people.

If something needs to change, I have the power to change it.

I am not afraid to say, "I'm sorry."

I also realize that other people are responsible for their own thoughts, words, choices, and actions.

7. Principle of Compassionate Service

I recognize the immense suffering in the world.

At the same time, I recognize that I can be of service.

Through empathy (being able to experience another person's situation by seeing the world through their eyes), I cultivate compassion which gives me the energy and inspiration to serve.

Then I no longer focus on the suffering and problems, but instead focus on the solutions and what I can do to help people.

These 7 Principles are the bedrock of Marketing With A Heart™...

People.

Purpose.

Profit.

PRINCIPLES.

(There's also a 5th "P", beyond Principles, which you'll discover at the end of this book.)

The New Bottom Line Means
Business (and Life) Success

I created Marketing With A Heart™ because the best way for businesses to make real impact in the world (and real profits) is to transform how they do marketing and selling: by cultivating trust, delivering value, and developing relationships.

Today, I'm grateful for the ongoing opportunity to speak, coach, lead seminars, and write...while serving the people who are committed to helping others: entrepreneurs, executives, speakers, authors, coaches, trainers, consultants, and other visionaries who are committed to making positive change in the world.

Now, how about *you*? Are you reaching the right audience, with the right language, and doing it the right way?

How you attract the right clients and partners to your business is not a mystery and not luck. It's the same with inspiring and influencing people to take action.

These are skills (you can learn) that must be implemented with consistency, discipline, a dash of fun, and a lot of heart.

This will lead people to naturally gravitate toward you and say yes to what you offer (vs. you having to chase after them).

If you don't learn these skills now, you'll have to make up for lost time, money, and energy that comes from not doing things consciously in the first place.

And, of course, there is a world of people who need your help right now.

There is no better day than today to start Marketing With A Heart™, and no better resource than this book.

I'm so glad you're here!

Join Me For A Quick Chat

First thing's first. Thank you very much for reading this!

I hope it helps you move your thinking and your business into more possibility, freedom, and impact, for yourself and others.

• Yes you can be more profitable by doing conscious marketing. Organizations and individuals that don't make this shift won't survive, because the market won't support them.

• Yes you can tell your story, use the right language, and deliver your message—to inspire, persuade, and transform lives.

• Yes you can run your business in a way that's aligned with your principles, so you can be more successful, have more fun, help more people, and be more fulfilled.

I want to support the good work that you're here to do...and help you do it full on. So I invite you to spend 15 or 20 peaceful minutes with me on the phone, Skype, or Google Hangout.

It helps me to understand what you're up to...so I can continue to serve you and others in the best ways possible. (Because you're probably dealing with the kinds of challenges that others are facing too.)

I'd love to give you my best advice. And I'm curious to know how this book has helped you. If you show up with your biggest challenge, I'll do my best to help you.

No obligation. Just win-win. More of us making a greater impact in the world. Visit marketingwithaheart.com/contact right now. We'll set up a time to chat and connect.

Looking forward to it!

Cheers,

Ben

Chapter 1
PEOPLE

Marketing is how you can change lives with your message. This is why the right kind of marketing is critical to your success. You'll discover perspectives and approaches to high integrity marketing, selling, and influence that are simple, powerful, and you can use right now.

31

Making Marketing Better By Making It Conscious

AS A PURPOSE driven leader, entrepreneur, executive, politician, speaker, author, coach, trainer, consultant, or other visionary who's committed to making positive change in the world, creating the greatest possible impact with your message is a direct result of your ability to connect deeply with people.

Connecting deeply happens by marketing, selling, and persuading with authenticity and integrity.

It's simply having a conversation where you care as much about what you say as the person you're speaking with.

There's one goal: to cultivate and develop relationships... whether it's with your audience, prospective clients, stakeholders, partners, or affiliates. And when relationships come from authenticity and integrity, amazing things happen.

There is an experience of real connection.

There is an opportunity for knowing, liking, and trusting, on both sides of the relationship.

There is also an opportunity for creating transformation while creating income.

You can help people remove the blocks that keep them from reaching their goals and achieving their dreams.

More importantly, these are the foundations of human connection that will remind everyone that we're all in this together.

And when people recognize that this is about all of us, then there is compassion and mutual support for everyone's highest good and success.

This is conscious marketing.

Making Marketing Better By Making It Conscious
Case Study

ROLAND IS A purpose driven leader who is doing conscious marketing. It's transformed how he creates content and speaks with people...which has helped him be happier, more productive, more successful, and more fulfilled.

"It's a conversation that benefits everyone," he began. "Instead of doing "marketing" and "selling" (which I used to hate), I shifted my perspective.

"I committed to having authentic conversations (through one-on-one dialogue, group interactions, and speeches...as well as written, audio, and video content).

"My goal: to communicate in such a way that I serve people, serve myself, and create the highest and best possible results for everyone, without being attached to a specific outcome.

"Because what happens is often better than I'd ever imagined.

The results are stupendous!

"I've developed relationships with partners that have allowed me to serve more people than I ever thought possible.

"I've created a space of mutual respect and trust. It's given my clients the confidence to step outside of who they think they are and into who they know they want to be.

"It's in this space that people can get unstuck and make positive changes that last a lifetime.

"I'm grateful to be able to share what I love with the world while making more money, which has transformed my business and my life."

Connecting The Dots So Everyone Can Win

WHETHER YOU'RE AN executive, entrepreneur, or elected official, you are a leader.

Conscious leadership is about shaping the future.

It's about persuading people to say yes to your vision or dream and being able to align it with a vision or dream of theirs.

Effective leadership ultimately comes down to cultivating trust...and to good marketing. Because conscious marketing is how you communicate with and influence people (prospects, customers, and clients) in a way that inspires them to take action.

Leadership is also how you communicate with and influence people in a way that inspires them to take action.

This can include prospects, customers, clients, vendors, partners, managers, stockholders, co-workers, employees, government, media, communities, and your board of directors.

What this means is that you need to communicate to each stakeholder uniquely and through the right channels.

Because all of these folks are more than just numbers on a spreadsheet.

This makes conscious marketing critical to your success.

Conscious marketing is what makes your prospects buy and your stakeholders buy in.

Whether you're promoting, presenting, partnering, or producing, sooner or later you'll want to align people with your vision and then inspire them to take action.

And the best part?

It's when you can do it in a way that's a win-win for everyone.

Connecting The Dots So Everyone Can Win
Case Study

I WAS RECENTLY having lunch with a prospective client, Mary, who is the founding partner of an executive coaching company.

She helps organizations implement a combination of conscious leadership, conscious culture, and Holacracy that results in more efficiency, better decision making, greater innovation, and a more positive working environment.

Her company is literally changing organizational culture.

But like any revolutionary concept, it can take awhile to become widely accepted. It often takes people a long time to change.

So we spoke about the most effective ways of marketing the concept to more organizations. First, we discussed communication. I asked her about her approach.

Was she speaking to the right organizations (the right audience), the ones who would be open to the discussion and who have specific needs that her company can meet?

For each of these organizations, did she understand what their primary fears, frustrations, needs, desires, motivations, goals, hopes, vision, and dreams are?

Did she tailor her marketing and presentation language to reflect this? When she spoke, did she empathize with the audience?

Did she connect the dots to show how her services are the fastest, simplest, most cost effective way for these organizations to eliminate their major challenges and achieve their goals?

(Well, now she would.)

Why You Want People To Like You…FAST

YEARS OF STUDY and research in psychology, sociology, biology, communication, marketing, and advertising offer consistent truths about your ability to influence and persuade.

Whether it's your prospect, customer, client, audience, or partner, your job is to help people get to know you, like you, trust you, see you as a credible authority, and understand that you're offering them value…so they will say yes to the action that you want them to take.

What's the fastest, most effective way to do all of this?

Empathy.

It's the most powerful, least understood, and least used tool for moving people into action.

Empathy is the capacity to experience another person's situation by seeing the world through their eyes.

When you're empathetic (and people recognize you are), an amazing thing happens.

They like you more.

They'll realize you've been listening to them.

When you listen deeply, you'll uncover their fears and pain as well as their hopes and dreams.

This will give you the right language to speak to them.

It will reveal what products/services/solutions to offer.

And it will help you create a tribe of people who say YES to you because you're helping them to realize their dreams.

Why You Want People To Like You...FAST
Case Study

AT A RECENT mastermind in L.A., the entire large group of us (conscious entrepreneurs, executives, transformational leaders, speakers, authors, and coaches) would periodically split off into smaller groups of 10 or so, to dig in deeper on a topic.

The topic was ethical persuasion.

How can you move a person, an audience, or an organization from from curious, to connected, to cooperative, and then finally to committed?

And how can you do it in a way that benefits everyone involved, so yes is the right choice, for all?

We went around the table.

I spoke about empathy.

"Empathy helps a person feel as if they know you (because we feel like we "know" the people who really listen to us).

"It helps a person trust you (they realize you "get them" because you've been speaking about their experience in their language).

"You're seen as a credible authority because you're able to offer a solution to their challenge and a way for them to realize their dreams (because you've listened deeply and understand what they actually need).

"When you use real empathy (no faking), a person will quickly come to like you.

"You will change their lives.

"And ultimately the world."

Why You Never, Ever Want To Close A Sale

WHEN YOU MAKE an offer to your potential clients, do it so they are fully committed to their choice to invest in you.

Or fully committed to not.

If you have a wishy washy commitment, the chances of them following through with your system or process are slim to none.

It will drain your energy, eat up your time, and leave them dissatisfied with their results.

To help people get fully committed (to yes or no), take these steps.

(And as you do, make sure you are listening very closely...so you can operate from a place of high integrity and with the intention of the best outcome for everyone involved.)

1. First, educate them (so they can make the right choice for their situation).

2. Next, over-deliver value (so you can impact their lives, regardless of whether they invest in you or not).

3. Finally, bring ethical persuasion and influence into the conversation (so you can help them take that leap, if it will truly serve them).

There's a difference between someone who is on the fence and someone who is hesitating because of a bigger issue.

Your job is to recognize the difference so you can support them in making the choice that's for everyone's highest good.

Why You Never, Ever Want To Close A Sale
Case Study

I WAS ALMOST finished with the teaching segment of my webinar "Helping Your Potential Clients Commit To Yes...Or No".

Before wrapping up the content and beginning my offer, I scanned the chat box.

I planned for Q&A at the end, but wanted to "take the audience's pulse" to see if there were any questions or comments that should be addressed sooner.

The first was a comment, which I read out loud.

"Every 'no' brings you closer to a 'yes'."

I agreed and dug in a little deeper when I responded.

"When you hear a 'no' it can mean that the person is not a good fit and it's better that the two of you don't work together.

"Conversely, a 'no' can also mean 'not now'.

"Both interpretations require a deeper understanding of your potential client's situation.

"That's why you never you want to try and "close" a sale. You want to have a conversation and listen deeply.

"And if you realize that 'no means not now', then you have the amazing opportunity to be a coach.

"You can help this person release their limiting beliefs so they can commit to working with you...and toward the results they want, that will transform their life."

Most People Only Put Out Fires, So Stop Hiring Them

WHEN YOU HIRE someone (an employee, consultant, vendor, or partner) would you rather have a person who reacts to problems, or a person who can discover the deeper issues... before they turn into time-, money-, and energy-sucking monsters?

Do you want someone who puts out fires or someone who can look deeply at an issue and discover what's really going on...then anticipate the opportunities and challenges?

- People try to sell products and services online.
- Mostly it doesn't work.
- So they hire a coach or a consultant.

The "problem solving" coach or consultant will try to fix something: suggesting more and different modes of advertising, a sleeker website, and a new social media strategy, for example.

The "problem finding" coach or consultant, however, will find the right problem to solve, which will save you time, energy, and money.

In this scenario the issue is often (too often), that the person or company created a product or service without doing the important, initial research.

You can have the best product or service ever, but if you don't identify what's motivating your audience (and the actual words they're using to talk about it), then you'll be putting out fires all day long.

Most People Only Put Out Fires, So Stop Hiring Them
Case Study

NOT LONG AGO...when magazines were holding their own, I lived in New York.

Over the years, I managed the print production of several titles...sometimes advertising, but more often editorial.

To move up the career ladder, I would start by interviewing with one high profile magazine or another. So would a lot of other people.

Every other candidate would talk about how well they solved problems.

I, on the other hand, would take out a dog-eared copy of the magazine (current issue) and point out every flaw: spelling errors, color reproduction issues, and sections where there were clearly advertising and editorial conflicts. From there, I would suggest solutions for the next issue.

While the editor or publisher would groan (and sometimes even curse) as I pointed these things out, I always got the job.

Because I was problem finding, not putting out fires.

Problem finding is about preventing the fires from starting in the first place.

Problem solving is a reaction to, well, a problem.

Don't get me wrong.

I want to honor and acknowledge problem solving. It is an important survival skill and critical in every business.

But do you want to just survive?

Or do you want to thrive?

Even If You Don't Know The 80/20 Rule, Do This

IF YOU WANT to help more people and make the money that you deserve, it's critical to identify, connect with, and get involved with people who are successful doing what you want to do.

(Or at least those folks who've done something similar enough.)

You want to model and learn from successful people.

And if possible, you want them as your coach, mentor, and/or to be part of a mastermind group.

Not only have these people already achieved what you want to do.

They also have the wisdom, experience, resources, and connections that will get you on the fast track.

This is the bridge between your great idea and your great outcome.

You've probably heard of the 80/20 rule.

You can learn 80% of what you need to know in 20% of the time by being coached, mentored, and joining a mastermind.

Just make sure to do your homework so you invest in the right people.

You will reach your goals faster (without all the wasted time, energy, and money) since you will learn what you really need, not what unethical marketers claim you need.

Investing in yourself like this means to invest in a new way of thinking.

You are investing in results, not just spending money.

Even If You Don't Know The 80/20 Rule, Do This

Case Study

MARK, A MEMBER of a mastermind group I'm in, was thinking about investing in a year long coaching program for speaking.

He had doubts so he invited me to lunch.

On a sheet of paper, we sketched out the pros and cons.

It was clearly a good idea to be mentored by someone whose focus is on building a speaking business instead of just what to do onstage.

It was also a way for Mark to realize his dream faster and to impact more people.

Mark worried that it would be "one more thing not to finish".

But when we analyzed his weekly schedule, we found slots that could be elegantly rearranged to make it work.

We also discussed money.

While it was more than he'd ever invested in his business, Mark realized that with strategic budgeting and a domestic vacation this year (vs. going abroad), that it would be tight, but doable.

As a result, Mark chose to invest in his success.

While writing this book, I got a call from Mark.

His speaking coach invited him up to the stage at a large bootcamp event.

He offered and sold enough coaching packages to cover his own coaching investment...and had enough left over to travel overseas.

Use Your Audience's Words To
Give Them Exactly What They Want

IF YOU WANT to connect and develop a relationship with your prospect, customer, client, or audience, you want to communicate in their language...with the words they are using to articulate their challenges, fears, frustrations, experiences, needs, values, hopes, and dreams.

You'll want to know as much about this person as you know about your best friend.

Your message needs to "speak" to one person at a time, even when you are reaching out to thousands.

You want each person to feel that they know you, like you, trust you, and that you are an authority or expert on your topic.

When you do this, you will create a shared human connection and experience.

You will reach them with your message and provide them with exceptional value.

Then you can create superior products and services (based on what they need, because they've told you). From there, you can make great offers so they'll want to invest in you and tell others about you.

If you don't do this, you'll waste time, money, and energy trying to reach people with a message that doesn't resonate with them or trying to talk them into buying something that they aren't looking for in the first place.

Use Your Audience's Words To
Give Them Exactly What They Want
Case Study

MARIA IS A "what if" learner.

She needs to imagine the outcomes of what she's learning as they will apply to her business and her life.

So I taught her how to write great marketing and sales copy through a simple process of conversation.

"Be sure to "speak" to one person and don't write like you're addressing a group.

"And remember about language: the more clear, concise, compassionate, and colloquial it is, the more effective it will be.

"Imagine this one person is your best friend...who experiences the whole range of joy, pain and everything in between...someone who wants to be happy, safe, healthy, and free (just like you).

"Picture having a heart to heart discussion...about their dreams and challenges...especially what keeps them up at night...what they can't get out of their heads.

"What words are they using?

"What emotions are coming up?

"Empathize with them, acknowledge them, and let them know that they are not alone, that it is ok, there is hope, and that you are the one who can help them.

"Teach them how to get past that pain or challenge both today, and for the long haul.

"Then show how they can reach their dreams as quickly and effectively as possible."

If You Don't Know This Phrase Your Business Will Fail

EVERY TIME YOU create any kind of content or presentation, imagine the person that you'll be speaking to...sitting in the audience or at the other end of the table.

Put yourself in their shoes. Ask "yourself" this question:

"What's in it for me?"

That's the starting point. What you're creating is not for or about you. It's about them.

They want to know, "what's in it for me"?

These are the **benefits** of what you're offering.

Why should they invest their time, energy, and/or money in you? Remember:

1. Benefits get people toward a goal, desire, or dream. Benefits also get people away from fear, pain, or discomfort.

2. Benefits should be concrete and create an experience. (Think of the difference between "fruit" and "a juicy red Gala apple, so perfectly sweet...you can feel the juice running down your chin when you take a bite...as you look out over the ocean on a breezy, summer day.")

3. The most powerful benefits touch the deepest emotions. (What's the driving force that motivates a person who wants to lose weight? Is it to be healthy, or is it to get a date because they are sad and lonely?)

The best content teaches people how to get away from fear/pain and achieve the dream/goal that they want.

Now, write yourself a note.

"What's in it for me?"

If You Don't Know This Phrase Your Business Will Fail Case Study

SHANI HAS A a food growing program for people who live in cities. Her next step is to sell products and group coaching.

I asked her to imagine…in specific detail, her best customer.

Then put herself in that person's shoes and ask, "What's in it for me?"

This would help her create the right content.

Each week, she'd shoot a 2 minute video for YouTube.

She would also use Twitter, Facebook, and Google+ to deliver quick tips that people can consume, comment on, like, and share.

This all will bring traffic to her blog where she can invite people to optin to her email list (by offering more valuable content).

Her optin content helps people quickly solve a problem with easy-to-digest information that they can understand and use right away.

In this case, it's "How To Grow Food For A Family of 4 On Your Fire Escape".

There's so much value that people will not only learn to grow food, but they will know, like, trust, and see Shani as an authority.

At the same time, it entices them to want more from her.

So when she offers products and group coaching, people are much more likely to make the investment in what she offers, happily.

Copywriting That Soars vs. Copy That Just Sucks

IF YOU WANT to write headlines, email, video, sales letters, and website copy that will persuade people to read, click, and invest in your products and services, you'll want to make sure they understand what's in it for them (benefits).

Most people's copywriting sucks because it focuses on the features of what they offer instead of the results (benefits) that their offer will deliver.

They spend hours and a ton of energy writing about features and put a ton of money into creating reports, books, and videos...all about features.

But nobody buys.

Nobody clicks.

Hardly anyone even reads.

And then comes the self doubt...wondering where it all went wrong...worrying about the money you've wasted...and thinking that maybe it would just be easier to give up.

Do you really want to go through all that?

By focusing on benefits (results) you connect the dots for your audience to show them how your product or service delivers the outcome they want.

And when you dig deeper and reveal the benefits of the benefits, you can articulate the underlying emotional experience of your prospects.

Because it's important to remember: "facts tell, emotions sell".

This is good copywriting.

When you know your audience, the language they use, and what's most important to them, it's easy.

Copywriting That Soars vs. Copy That Just Sucks
Case Study

I WAS HELPING my client Elaine understand the differences among features, benefits, and ultimate benefits (benefits of the benefits).

"Imagine that you are selling a map with all the beaches in California.

"If you were writing about **features,** you'd say:

"*'This map has colors, topography, distance and other information.'*

"If you were writing about the **benefits,** you'd say:

"*'With this map, you can choose the beach you want...since you'll know how far to drive, the amenities, and what kind of people to expect.'*

"If you then added **ultimate benefits** (which are the underlying emotional reasons), you might say:

"*'Best of all, because you can choose YOUR beach, you'll be able to have the experience that YOU want.*

"*'You can enjoy valuable time with your spouse and kids...because with how busy life is these days, you don't get so many opportunities like this.*

"*'And the kids, wow, they're growing up so fast. Pretty soon they'll be off on their own...*

"*'So I invite you to invest in yourself and your family by getting this map today...so you can immediately begin to create an experience and memory that you and your family will love and remember, for a lifetime.'"*

Smart People Often Write Wrongly and Worser

MOST SMART PEOPLE don't write the same way they speak. Instead, they write like they are submitting a PhD to a thesis committee. The results?

Nobody reads. Nobody buys.

Lots of wasted time, money, and energy.

(This is not good for your business.)

When you create any kind of content...whether it's an email, blog post, speech, video, Facebook post, webinar, information product...basically anything...you want to people to consume it and share it.

So you want to communicate in a way that people understand, and makes them realize that you understand them. You want to describe their challenge or desired outcome better than they can.

But for some reason, the vast majority of smart people learned how to write...the wrong way.

Writing needs to be clear, concise, compassionate, and colloquial, so you can:

1. connect with people, at their deepest emotional level;

2. instantly create rapport...so you can help them know, like, trust, and view you as a credible authority;

3. invite them to take action that will help them (whether to click a link or buy your book or sign up for coaching with you, etc.); and

4. deliver valuable information that provides a powerful transformation in a person's life.

Smart People Often Write Wrongly and Worser
Case Study

JORGE IS A dynamic and dynamite motivational speaker. The first time I saw him live I was riveted. He delivered the perfect combination of information, inspirational quotes, benefits, and stories that made his teaching come alive and stick in the minds and hearts of the audience.

Jorge's biggest challenge was getting people to subscribe to his email list, even though he offered an incredibly high value training at no cost. He had almost no optins. So he asked me to take a look.

I did "quick and dirty" analysis of his content: the copy on his website, in his emails, on his Facebook posts, and on his landing page. His biggest issues (which are pervasive among "experts" and "authorities" when they create content and marketing copy) were:

- Too many words.
- Too many big words.
- Too many ideas.
- Too complex and abstract.
- Too many tangents and sidebars.
- Too many long sentences with too many commas.
- Too little focus on the tangible, immediate benefits and core, emotional "ultimate" benefits.

So I offered a "quick and dirty" solution. Instead of writing… create an outline (like for a speech), record it, transcribe it, publish it, and repurpose it multiple ways.

Why Do They Run When The Doors Start Closing?

DID YOU EVER notice how people casually walk toward the elevator?

But as soon as they see the doors closing, they run?

This is a perfect analogy for the psychological influence triggers of urgency and scarcity.

There is only one elevator (at least for the moment) and there's suddenly a deadline to get inside.

It's critical to use these triggers in your marketing, selling, and influence because you want to help people take action.

Deadlines create urgency and limited quantities (or space) create scarcity.

It also helps when you frame urgency in the context of an idea, theme, holiday, or story (your birthday, International Hug Day, your big epiphany, etc.)

Consider this...

You're selling a program you've already offered, but now at a discount.

And your sale will only be three days long (so you don't have to do any major marketing ahead of time).

Pick a reason that will get people's attention.

Tell them what you're offering, the price, why you're doing this now, that there are limited quantities (as long as it's true), and why.

Email them once each day (over the three days) to trigger urgency and scarcity.

Often, it's in the last 6 hours that 50% of your sales will happen.

Why Do They Run When The Doors Start Closing?
Case Study

CANDICE AND I were strategizing how to use urgency and scarcity (ethically) to test a new idea.

She wanted to offer a four week training program.

I recommended that she write the sales page (which articulates the framework, features, benefits, and ultimate benefits of the program), but not to create the content.

She would promote the training for 3 days: Thursday, Friday (Valentine's Day), and Saturday. It would start Monday.

Candice let people know about the program and why: because of a challenge she kept noticing with most of her clients, she wanted to create a product that would solve it.

(And Valentine's Day was the perfect time.)

She shared why she would offer a 50% discount: since she planned to create the program via webinar (to have the energy of a live audience) there might be a few hiccups in the production quality.

Candice also offered a free bonus: the first 10 people to sign up would receive a one hour coaching call.

The beauty of this strategy is twofold:

1. If nobody signs up, she doesn't have to create anything.

2. If enough people invest, she can create the content week by week and make real time adjustments based on the participant's feedback.

Mirror Mirror, On The Wall...

PERSONAL RESPONSIBILITY IS the key to success in business, in your life, and your capacity to help others.

True power arises from taking personal responsibility for your life, knowing yourself, and continuing to discover who you are and why you're here.

This is the power that comes from your guiding principles of truth, integrity, responsibility, and love.

What choices have you made in the past?

What was important to you then?

How about now?

How have your choices brought you to this moment, to this version of yourself, and to these circumstances?

Additionally, your perspectives, history, principles, strengths, and areas of improvement can give you an indication of who you can be...and what you still may need to overcome to get there.

When you take a good look at yourself (although it can be difficult sometimes), there are gifts of learning and discovery you may not have known or expected...because you're asking questions you may never have thought, wanted to, or had the courage to ask.

Taking the time for this personal inquiry will give you the opportunity to expand your talents, vision, and strengths while eliminating and/or understanding how best to work with your areas of improvement.

(And as far as these areas of improvement...you can partner with someone whose strengths these are. You can also outsource many of them!)

Mirror Mirror, On The Wall...
Case Study

AT A NETWORKING event the other night, I was in the middle of a conversation about responsibility and success.

When I had the chance to share, I made the connection to principles.

"As you follow your guiding principles and take responsibility for your life, you will continue to grow, be happier, and make an even greater impact in the world.

"You are responsible for how you communicate: through your words, your body language, in your marketing, when making the sale, as you lead others, and in your life.

"You are responsible for who you are and how you deal with the events and circumstances that you experience.

"You can react and blame, or you can respond, proactively.

"And when you make a mistake, you can forgive yourself.

"You are responsible for everything in your life...and to do what's right for yourself, your relationships, your health, your career, and your happiness.

"You are responsible for your thoughts, fears, doubts, and judgements.

"It doesn't mean that they won't show up. It does mean that you can choose how they will affect you.

"Will you make them bigger?

"Or will you acknowledge them (with gratitude for what you will learn), and let them go?"

The Most Peaceful Way To Give Fear The Finger

BEING AN ENTREPRENEUR, starting a new business, restructuring an organization, or entering a new market can bring up all kinds of fear every day.

Psychologists say that we're born with only two fears: falling and loud noises.

We've learned the rest.

Fear can show up as anxiety, nervousness, lethargy, anger, doubt, and/or procrastination.

Regardless, there's always a physical component.

Pay attention, you can literally feel the fear in your body.

If you observe the sensations (like a scientist), and breathe deeply (without judging or creating stories that make the fear bigger and more unpleasant), then the sensations of the fear will only last for about 90 seconds.

By objectively observing the physical feelings, you interrupt the fear patterns in your brain and your body.

What this means is that you can stop reacting and start responding to fear instead.

So when you're writing your blog, recording a video, cultivating a client, speaking, running a meeting, or whatever else brings up fear...you can now breathe, feel the fear, and do it anyway.

Everything that you experience will teach you what you need to do next.

Fear is a powerful teacher that can activate you.

Make it your ally so you can succeed in your business and help more people.

The Most Peaceful Way To Give Fear The Finger
Case Study

WHEN I FIRST met Lee, he called himself an "intellectual, terrified, sometimes fearless, perfectionist".

As a person in the public eye most of his adult life, he's been attempting to manage fear for years.

The difficulty is that his first response is to try and talk himself out of fear. He tries to avoid facing his fear by being a perfectionist.

The results are mixed and inconsistent because it's really hard to use your brain to stop your thoughts.

So we developed a personalized approach.

First, when he notices fear, he takes 3 long, deep breaths while feeling the sensations in his body.

If the fear is especially powerful, he'll repeat the 3 breaths while staying focused on the physical feelings. He'll also monitor his perfectionism.

Then, depending on the situation, he'll say (or whisper to himself) one or a combination of the following:

1. "Breathing into fear is like exercising. I build this muscle every day."

2. "I'll get things right, faster, if I just do them. I learn best by doing, adjusting, and doing some more."

3. "Imperfect action always beats perfect inaction."

4. "Winning is simple. It's means getting up each time I fall."

5. "I may die tomorrow, so I'm going to take my shot today. People need my help right now."

Marketing With A Heart™ | Coaching With Heart

If you're an executive, entrepreneur, politician, speaker, author, coach, trainer, consultant, or other visionary who's committed to making positive change, I invite you to explore coaching with me.

I'm committed to helping you share your message, gifts, and talents so they nourish your soul, support your lifestyle, and allow you to create a powerful impact in the world.

If you're not yet in a place where everything in your business is working in a way that's rewarding at every level, I'd like to personally support you and help you make that leap.

Marketing With A Heart™ has been helping individuals and organizations become more successful for almost 10 years (even though I only figured out the name a few years ago).

I'm honored and grateful to share this gift with the world, so we can all help more people, make more money, and live our lives how we want.

There is a very special moment that I want to share with you. It's that feeling of freedom. It's when your business and life begin to take on a whole new dimension. It's when possibilities unfold, profits increase, and peace prevails.

Why?

Because your business is expressing your core principles. It's who you are. Your marketing, selling, and communication truly become service...and continue to bring new and repeat business to your door.

Does this sound good to you?

Great! I invite you to find out more today by visiting marketingwithaheart.com/coaching

Chapter 2
PURPOSE

It's the "why" that fuels your passion and your mission. It's the strategy for making your dreams into reality. It's how you balance your long-term vision with day-to-day action so you can inspire, persuade, and transform lives.

Changing Your Perspective Will Change Lives

IF YOU WANT to succeed in business, help more people, make more money, and be an effective communicator, you'll want perspectives that serve you.

How you think and act has brought you the outcomes you're experiencing right now.

You are free to choose new perspectives anytime, especially when they aren't bringing you the experiences and results that you want.

Choose the right perspective on marketing, selling, and service.

When you do this, you can get your message in front of the right people and offer them the products and services they want (and will change their lives).

You will make the money you deserve...so you can create the business and life that you want...and help even more people.

Choose to communicate in a way that people will know you, like you, trust you, view you as an authority, and then be inspired to take action.

Serve the people who you know, like, and trust as well.

Stay on their radar by interacting with them regularly and giving them ongoing value...so they'll happily invest in your products and services and tell other people about the great work that you're doing.

Choose to stop being perfect.

Otherwise your dream will never happen.

Changing Your Perspective Will Change Lives
Case Study

WHEN I CREATED the Marketing With A Heart™ philosophy, I shared it with one of my masterminds.

The group is an amazing array of savvy entrepreneurs, executives, and other thought leaders who care deeply about service.

People were excited to finally have the language and system to align who they are with how they want to be in the world, especially in business.

At last, an opportunity to connect the head and the heart!

The more head-centered people in the group resonated strongly with the concept that marketing, selling, and persuasion (with a heart) is what you do FOR people: educating, over-delivering value, ethical influence, and changing lives.

They recognized how to immediately integrate "what you do FOR people" into their copywriting, product creation, speaking, marketing, advertising, internal communication, and who they chose as affiliates and joint venture partners.

The more heart-centered people resonated very strongly as well.

They recognized that marketing and selling are service, since they can help people be happier, more successful, and more fulfilled.

Additionally, if they will offer something that will change lives, it's their responsibility to let people know about it.

Otherwise they will be doing a disservice.

Manipulation Bad. Ethical Influence Good.

MANIPULATION IS GETTING someone to think, speak, or act in a way that will benefit you but isn't going to benefit them.

Many people consider selling to be a form of manipulation. As a result, many people think that selling is bad.

We have a lifetime of cultural stereotypes, media messaging, and crappy "sales" experiences that support this.

I offer a contrary perspective.

Selling is service.

And it happens through conversation.

You *do* want people to invest in your stuff, because you know that it will help them.

So it's your responsibility to help them understand if it's right for them.

And sometimes they just don't realize how much they actually need it.

This is where persuasion, or ethical influence, is critical.

You want to educate people so you can help them make informed choices that will have a positive impact on their lives.

This also creates the opportunity for them to know, like, trust, and view you as a credible authority.

And if you're doing this from a place of high integrity (and I know you are), you are giving this person an amazing deal and opportunity to change their experience (now), and create a lasting transformation over their lifetime.

Manipulation Bad. Ethical Influence Good.
Case Study

TONY OWNS A consulting company that helps socially responsible businesses get more profitable so they can fulfill their missions.

We got on the phone for about five minutes yesterday.

It was right before his presentation: an interactive, high value, no cost training (for staff and board members) that was wrapped up with an invitation to partner for a year.

Tony wanted to feel great about the conversation he was about to have.

So I reminded him…

"First, take a deep breath.

"People don't want to be "sold" but they do want to be educated so they can make informed investments.

"You know what they're going through. You've been there: the challenges, the opportunities, and the places where people can get stuck.

"You know that what you're offering has helped you and has helped other organizations earn 10 times their investment in you, every year since hiring you.

"You are offering your knowledge, experience, and expertise in a way that is going to deliver the same outcomes…if they'll follow your guidance.

"You're not selling what you offer.

"You're selling the results that you'll bring to the organization (and the people they serve) which is worth so much more than the investment you're asking for."

Marketing Is Your Right And Your Responsibility

MARKETING AND SELLING are powerful conversations that can make massive positive impact in people's lives.

Marketing is service.

It's how you deliver your message to the people who need it.

It's how you communicate and inspire by giving life-changing information and value.

While you can change one life through your message, you can change the world through your marketing.

Marketing allows you to leverage both your time and your relationships so you can help more people.

Selling is service because it's a way to transform lives.

You can provide the information, products, and opportunities people need and that can help them reach their goals and achieve their dreams.

You've lived in such a way that you've got an abundance of work and life experience.

You can inspire and instruct other people with what you know...whether it's how to improve their personal lives, how to achieve more in their professional lives, or how to build their own business.

If you believe that what you offer can truly help people, you have every right (and responsibility) to let them know about it and how much value it can give them...as well as the people they love.

Marketing Is Your Right And Your Responsibility
Case Study

ANGIE AND I were discussing her leadership coaching practice. She wanted to build her email list as well as offer group coaching and a subscription to a monthly continuity program (as an addition to her one-on-one services).

She was hesitant about marketing, selling, and charging the right price for what she offers…which are the results that she brings to people's lives.

My response was this:

"…In fact, what you are selling is unique. That's right, you are the only one in the world who can deliver it, because it is based on you.

"You are selling your years of experience, education, failures and triumphs, insights and wisdom, time and energy, effort and talent…the essence of your expertise.

"It is profoundly valuable and you deserve to be compensated fairly and well for it.

"And think of all the people who truly need what you offer.

"Now, imagine what your life will be like…

"You are financially free because you've been sharing what you love with the world.

"Imagine what this has done for your career, your life, and the people you've been committed to helping…

"And since you've been doing all this from a place of service, you've never had to "sell" anything. You've only had to serve."

Where Does The Magic Really Happen?

WHAT IS MOST important to you?

Freedom?

Creativity?

Making a difference?

Having fun?

This is an incredibly important question and I'm asking you for two reasons.

First, it's imperative to know what drives you. Second, there are times when you will find yourself out of sync with your guiding principles.

When this happens, you can easily become unhappy with your work and incredibly unproductive.

Having this awareness is critical when you want to help people live happier, more productive, peaceful lives...and make the money you deserve.

It starts with putting a stake in the ground, today, and saying what your passion is, what makes you the happiest, and how you want to help people.

It's also being willing to expand your comfort zone by 10% and staying open to opportunities that will show up in different forms (and at different times) than you expect.

A big part of this whole journey and adventure is faith (in yourself and beyond yourself). Be willing to trust that you will figure it out as you go along.

You will achieve your dreams in a practical way, so you can make the money that you deserve...and be more fulfilled...while honoring what's important and true to you.

Where Does The Magic Really Happen?
Case Study

MOUNIR THOUGHT SHE was the victim of corporate downsizing. But in our chats, she began shifting her perspective from crisis to opportunity...recognizing that her job never gave her real satisfaction and the layoff was actually a gift.

She was now free to do what she loves and according to her own rules.

She was still freaked out about starting a business, so began asking me questions about websites, marketing, products, and coaching programs.

I asked her to pause and take a breath. Then I invited her to start with the foundations.

"Who are you?

"Where/What is the edge of your comfort zone?

"What inspires you?

"What makes you curious and passionate?

"What's most important to you?

"When you are clear about this, you can make sure that whatever you're doing is always inspired and aligned with your guiding principles.

"When you're in that space, you'll find a way to handle all the marketing, selling, persuasion, and business components.

"In the meantime, you can find ways to bring value to the people who appreciate your passion and vision and have a need for the answers you can give them.

"But they don't have the time, energy, skills, or desire to discover them on their own.

"Most likely, this will be your niche."

The Most Powerful Force That Drives Your Business

WHEN YOU WANT to create results with your marketing and in your business, you want to start with your "why".

Your "why" is what's important to you and how you want to live your life. It's based on your principles and part of your code of conduct.

It's who you are.

Being who you are—completely, courageously, compassionately, and without apology—is the greatest gift that you can offer.

From there comes your message, your service, your brand, and your vision of what's possible.

When your vision is clear you don't need to get sidelined by the inevitable challenges that show up.

You can stay focused on your goals and take the steps to get there, every day.

Knowing who you are and knowing your "why" is also the driving force behind your story.

People will respond to your marketing, engage with you, and ultimately invest in your products and services because of your story.

Your story starts the conversation.

It opens the door for people to know you, like you, trust you, see you as an authority, and receive the value that you offer them.

Your story makes your marketing, selling, persuasion, and leadership more effective, so you can generate more sales, make more money, and help more people.

The Most Powerful Force That Drives Your Business
Case Study

WHEN I WORK with clients, some are clear about their "why" and their story. Others need to get clear.

The biggest component of both "why" and someone's story is their personal vision: who they want (and need) to become to be more fulfilled, design their life, make more money, and impact more people.

So I guide them through the following process to remind them that their story and their "why" is evolving, just like they are. I invite them to reflect.

"Who do you want to be?

"How do you want to live?

"What do you want your business to look like?

"Who do you want to serve?

"When do you want it all to happen?"

"Be specific as you clarify your vision and set your intentions. Write them on index cards, make a vision board, or create a multi-sensory vision board (which is a slideshow of your vision board images set to music that inspires you).

"Say your affirmations aloud twice each day. Use all your senses and make the experience tangible and emotional.

"Smile.

"Then take action today to create the future you want.

"But don't get attached to one specific outcome. There's a good chance that it will be even more amazing than you've imagined."

Stepping Backwards To Future Success

FOR YEARS I'VE been learning about and experimenting with different ways to get things done effectively, while moving toward my dreams.

I want to share a favorite with you, which I learned from one of my coaches, James Malinchak.

1. Define your outcome. Make it specific and tangible, with a due date and time. Create a vision board. Look at it more than once each day.

2. Understand why. What's the purpose? Focus on the benefit, the results that it will bring, to you and others. This is critical because there will be challenges along the way.

(Remember, the bigger your "why" the easier the "how".)

3. Ask yourself who can help you reach this outcome. Contact them right away. Consider how you can serve them.

4. Use future perfect planning. Envision success. Then, from that point of success, start to "look" backwards...to the step immediately before the success...then the step immediately before that, etc....until right now.

5. What could get in the way? What solutions can you have ready? How can you succeed before you even take the first step?

6. Take action NOW! Do it immediately. Start your momentum...

7. Celebrate your successes!

(The big ones and the small ones, each day).

Stepping Backwards To Future Success
Case Study

KAREN IS A baby boomer with a child, grandchild, and elderly father at home.

After 25 years in the corporate world, she retired to stay sane, support her family, and start her own consulting business.

The challenge was working at home.

So I offered some coaching.

"Your mind, heart, and the people around you are all ready to help you realize your dreams.

"So make sure you create the circumstances and choose the perspectives that will lead you...without stopping...to the outcome you want...and support you every single day of the journey.

"Part of it is acceptance: allowing, attracting, and being open to what you need to make your dream come true, even if it's not what you expect.

"The other part is not letting your inner critic take over.

"Give yourself the logical reasons that will make it inevitable for you to succeed.

"Especially since you are your own boss...create accountability by pretending that you have to go to work to earn your pay everyday.

"Have the attitude, 'how can I be worth 10X what they invest in me?'

"Be gentle, nurturing, and care for yourself.

"But keep the balance otherwise you will enable yourself to not get things done."

Do It! Did It! Dance! Do It Again!

ONE OF THE biggest challenges is getting stuff done. This method will yield incredible results if you follow the instructions. You'll be amazed.

Science teaches us that we have periods of energy and focus each day that last for about 90 minutes (or so). Then we need to rest, recover, and recharge.

Here is the method:

50 minutes (focused task);

10 minutes (break);

50 minutes (focused task);

40 minutes (break/celebrate!);

(total 2.5 hours)

[Repeat.]

Here are the details:

1. Use a timer.

2. During the 50 minute "focused tasks", do one thing only. Don't answer the phone, check email, surf the web, or take a break. Set your intention at the beginning, start the timer, and go. (Note: "one thing" could mean returning several phone calls, for example.)

3. During the breaks, do something that is energetically different. For example, if you've been working on the computer (mental), do something physical (yoga) or emotional (calling a friend). You will recover your energy much more quickly by switching among mental/physical/emotional activities.

Even if you only do one of these blocks each day...you'll likely get more things done than you ever have before.

(Ok, go schedule your first block right now!)

Do It! Did It! Dance! Do It Again!
Case Study

JOSE HELPS NONPROFITS with strategic planning and recognizes that many don't have the budget for a consultant. So we sketched out an offer that many nonprofits would take advantage of: a strategic planning mastermind program with a training component, group coaching, and monthly calls.

Even with almost 20 years of experience, José knew he needed to write a book.

This would position him as an expert and help get his foot in the door with organizations.

He tried writing for months.

But each time he sat down, the phone rang, emails arrived, and his kids texted.

So even his "writing time" became just another fire drill.

So we formulated a plan for the next 90 days.

José would go to bed one hour earlier and wake up two hours earlier. This is where we scheduled his daily block of focused productivity time.

His family would be asleep, then involved in their own morning routines. His clients wouldn't be calling either.

And I made him promise that he wouldn't check email or Facebook until the block of time was complete.

In less than 90 days, he finished his book!

It was the key to getting more clients into his strategic planning mastermind.

The book also helped him get clear on the structure and delivery of his program.

This Isn't For Normal People

BECAUSE YOU'RE READING this, I know you're not normal. Thank you for that.

You have a unique combination of talent, knowledge, skills, education, ability, experience, vision...and the baseline desire to make a difference in the world with the gift that is your life.

You are here to learn and to grow, so you can access the full potential inside of you and share that with the world.

And to have fun!

This gives you the amazing opportunity to live a bigger life, do more, impact more people, and leave an amazing legacy.

The more you step into your power, the more people you can help.

And as you continue to step into this place, you take on a greater responsibility.

More people are investing their time, money, energy, and heart with you.

At the same time, you are responsible to and for yourself.

Serving others does not mean sacrificing yourself, your body, your family, or your happiness.

You are in charge of maintaining a balance among all of the key components of your life: work, health, mission, spirituality, family, legacy (or whatever you choose as your mix for your life).

You serve others best by serving yourself first.

This Isn't For Normal People
Case Study

YOLANDA DESCRIBES HERSELF as an "all or nothing" person who puts everyone else's needs before her own.

This has been one of our biggest challenges/opportunities in working together...helping her to make more sustainable choices, for her business and her life.

Yolanda had many success habits in place when we started.

She is committed to her goals, keeps a consistently positive focus, and has both a marketing and entrepreneurial mindset.

We built on those mindsets and went further.

Yolanda is learning how to regularly clear the emotional, physical, and mental clutter that can create tension.

She's developed rituals to optimize her focus, her physical health, and her productivity.

She understands how to assess her highest priority goals (clients/sales/outcomes/lifestyle/income/health/relationships/ etc.) and that she needs to take action on each of them every day.

Yolanda has learned how to make decisions from where she wants to be, not just where she is now, while considering her wellbeing in every choice that she makes.

She realizes that by growing and developing her mind, knowledge, and personal experiences...the richer she will be.

Yolanda has made an important choice.

Instead of hiring an average coach, she has invested an extraordinary coach, the right one for her.

Long Term Planning Is A Waste of Your Time

HAVE YOU EVER heard people who recommend making 5 and 10 year plans?

I'm not one of those people.

In my experience, everyone who makes 5 and 10 year plans in a dynamic, evolving environment (which is where most of us are) has to change those plans every 3 to 6 months.

Don't get me wrong.

It's vital to have a big picture vision AND to know that it may or may not work out.

The goal is to work on developing the skills that make the outcomes possible.

It's not about knowing the exact outcome. It's about holding the intentions and keeping the vision alive.

It's also about being flexible, because in most cases the outcome that you thought you wanted isn't what you really wanted, or it changes in some form: different audience, different business model, different timeframe, different life.

So go with the inspiration for the moment.

Go with the things that you are most interested in...and curious about...and fascinated and obsessed with.

Then get an idea of what you want to happen.

Then research the market to see if you can make your inspiration into something that will help people, make you money, and be fun and fulfilling.

Long Term Planning Is A Waste of Your Time
Case Study

NICK SPENT THREE years developing a successful business that he loves.

As he continued to serve his clients he discovered an opportunity that was a radical departure from his current situation.

He could serve more people, make more money, and work less.

When we got on the phone, he was going back and forth about doing it, because there was some risk involved.

I suggested that if he was inspired and believed that this was the path to follow, then he should allow himself to do it.

And to follow it wholeheartedly, passionately, jubilantly, and of course, practically.

Then let the doors open where they may...

I asked about the next 6-12 months.

Did he have a sense of enough certainty (among his inspiration, research, client feedback, intuition, and savings account) that this would be something he'd want to invest his time, money, and energy in?

Finally, I asked if he was attached to the outcome.

Because if he could recognize that success happens every single day (so he could enjoy the journey as well as the goal), then I knew he'd be more likely to succeed.

And his possibilities would be even greater than he imagined.

More Stress and Less Time With The People You Love

DO KNOW THE secret for creating reliable, predictable, sustainable results in your business and in your life?

It's having systems.

Consider the letters in the word s.y.s.t.e.m.: Save YourSelf Time, Energy, and Money.

Then consider this: the amount of stress you experience is directly related to the lack of systems you have.

And take it a step further. A system doesn't have to be complex.

By definition, it's just a series of components that combine to create a whole.

Or a series of steps that lead to an outcome.

If you do the same things each morning, your routine is a system.

How you bake a cake is a system.

Effective marketing is a system.

Conscious leadership is a system.

The beauty of a system is that it can take a large amount of friction out of any process because it reduces the amount of thinking.

If you have a system in place for exercise, there's a lot less opportunity for thinking, internal resistance, struggle, or not following through...because you repeat the same sequence at the same time each day.

You get it done, stay healthy, and save your willpower for other challenges and opportunities in your life.

More Stress and Less Time With The People You Love
Case Study

WHEN I STARTED working with Gertrude, I spoke about the benefits of systems and how they apply to marketing, selling, persuasion, and making a difference in people's lives. She already had some systems in place that supported her business and her life.

I helped her go further.

First, I pointed out that her market research, lead generation, sales funnel, launch sequence, and product development are all systems.

Additionally, picking her kids up from school and coordinating with her husband for dinner and homework is a system too.

With those perspectives in mind, we looked at what else could be systematized in Gertrude's business and life. We started with administration.

What was she doing (herself) that she could capture the steps and then turn over to an assistant or outsourcer?

The biggest one was email.

The system we established was for her assistant to manage her inbox and divide the messages 3 ways:

1) what the assistant could handle/answer herself;

2) all the items Gertrude needed to address (but could receive as a compiled list at the end of each day); and

3) items that needed to be handled right away, which the assistant would forward and clearly identify.

Think Less So You Can Get More Done

YOU WANT TO be organized, so you can create the habits and patterns that allow you to be productive, creative, resourceful, and successful, on a consistent basis.

Very often, people who say they are "creative" or "busy" have the most resistance to getting organized.

But organization actually creates the opportunities for more creativity and more time.

It's also more fun because you can reduce the stress that happens when you don't have plans, schedules, and systems.

You literally don't have to think as much, and you can focus more on your gifts and talents.

Being organized also allows you to grow your business and make more money, because success never happens when you're alone.

It comes from adding more people into the mix: an assistant, a partner, an affiliate, and/or an entire team.

You want to be organized so these people can easily plug in and help you reach the outcomes you want, faster.

If you don't get organized, you will be your own bottleneck, which will limit other people's ability to support you.

It will keep you from reaching all the people who truly need your help.

Getting organized is also key for spending more time with the people you love.

Think Less So You Can Get More Done
Case Study

EPHRAIM HAS AN amazing story: the only child of Ugandan immigrants, he came to the US when he was 5.

He taught himself to read English, got a scholarship to Juilliard, and spent the next 10 years as a guest musician for many high profile projects, but not his own.

His talent was amazing.

His drive, unstoppable.

He was ready to tour with his own band (thanks to the financial kickstart of a few allies).

He needed to hire a manager, someone who was extremely organized, resonated with his vision, and would lead the band in a way that allowed each member to focus on the music and trust that the "business" was being handled.

I made two recommendations.

First, the band members would need to support the array of necessary, routine tasks (rehearsals, sound checks, health and wellness, and media appearances) so life on the road would be smooth and produce extraordinary results.

Second, he needed to find a manager who could coordinate a variety of details, ideas, energies, and styles...while being clear on his vision and what he wants from this person.

As a result, Ephraim was able to hire a manager who helped the band move to the next level and beyond.

If You're A People Pleaser You Will Get Pooped On

CONSIDER THIS.

97% of the people who read a sales letter (or watch a sales video) don't buy.

And that 3% who do buy is considered success.

So whenever you're faced with making major changes in you packaging, your product, your marketing funnel, etc., be sure that the reason comes from a substantial or at least statistically significant number of occurrences (customer feedback, for example).

If you are only hearing a concern or objection from a few people, it's good to take that as a data point.

It's not necessarily time to do anything about it...until it becomes statistically significant or at least meaningful in terms of your results.

Of course you want everybody to be happy, so you want to take care of issues as soon as they come up.

But in reality, you're not going to make everybody happy all the time.

(You can always count on some number of people unsubscribing, canceling, or asking for a refund. That's the way it goes.)

If you choose to make a change, first think about what you can do in your marketing to address the concern.

Sometimes just articulating why you've done something the way you've done it and showing your audience the value and benefit will overcome their objection.

If You're A People Pleaser You Will Get Pooped On Case Study

BERNADETTE IS AN educational speaker. She asked how I would choose between offering a digital or physical product.

I recommended starting with digital (for speed of production and cost savings), especially since it's a new product.

Here's what I advised:

"If you deliver a physical product then you can't make updates as often.

"Your customers will have to pay more and wait longer because of manufacturing and shipping. International customers may have to pay additional costs as well.

"Make sure your sales funnel educates people about all of this.

"It's not just about the product but also about the method of delivery. Pre-sell and address all of the influence and decision making elements so you can overcome objections beforehand.

"Connect your audience with the value, even before you make the offer.

"If you get feedback requesting a physical product, ask yourself, 'does this feedback represent enough people in my audience that it's something I need to address right now?

"'Or could it be a concern in the future?'

"Then, if the feedback can be legitimately addressed through education and marketing, that's a better alternative than overhauling a process, creating new products, and investing major time, money, and energy."

How To Kill The Business Killer

DISTRACTION IS A motivation, progress, and business killer. You can't ignore it, and you do need to handle it.

How? Just focus on the next 30 days.

Then you don't have to think about all the other things coming down the road...and all the bright, shiny objects.

Whatever comes up (if it's not immediately relevant), mark it down on a piece of paper, or put it on your calendar, so you can deal with it at some point in the future.

That allows you to be in the present moment and to feel more in control because now you have a scope of work that feels manageable.

And you can (ideally) see it on one sheet of paper.

You can look at your list and recognize that you will reach these specific outcomes in a couple of weeks or a month.

Then you can set your priorities.

And because you have a long term vision, you know that if you take care of these priorities, you're certain to get to your goal.

Keep using your 30 day priorities as your filter.

If something comes up that doesn't immediately support this set of goals, put it on the calendar for the future. Or ignore it completely. Don't just collect stuff.

Otherwise there's too much diffuse energy, and too much "being busy" instead of choosing actions that progressively move you closer and closer to your goals.

So, what are you going to do for the next 30 days?

How To Kill The Business Killer
Case Study

I WAS EATING dinner with a potential client who I met at a speaking bootcamp.

I asked what his business goals are.

"I want to do a million dollar launch!"

"But," I responded gently, "you don't have a list yet."

He frowned, took a deep breath, and invited me to say more.

"Often, when people have that kind of big vision, they may feel overwhelmed when they think about all of the things they "should" be doing.

"I find it helpful to look at where I am right now and use the big vision as long term inspiration for where I want to go.

"But I just focus on what can I do right now to move me closer.

"You don't have a list. So before anything else, get a list.

"How do you do that? Get an optin page up first.

"And what do you need for that? A compelling, valuable offer.

"So get your offer together. For that, you need to know your audience.

"So figure that out. Chunk it down until you get to the very first steps.

"You know that when you start with a list, your million dollar launch becomes much more possible."

THE IDEAL SPEAKER FOR YOUR EVENT Live or Online

"When it comes to your attendees reaching their best...it's the inside game that leads to the outside win. I help audiences realize that each one of them is a leader (regardless of their profession or position)...and then show them how to inspire one person, or transform the lives of millions!"

—Ben Gioia, Marketing With A Heart™

Dear Event or Meeting Planner,

I understand that planning a meeting is like being a leader. In today's economy, getting a return on your investment is more important than ever. And doing it in a way that maximizes value for everyone involved is a win-win.

This is why my talk is designed to inspire and offer value to your audience...so they can create greater income and impact in the world.

As a highly in-demand speaker and bestselling author, I've presented to audiences around the country, around the world, and on the web...ranging from intimate groups of 10, to events with 500+ attendees.

I am available for keynotes (opening and closing), conferences (breakout sessions, workshops, educational trainings), business or community events, retreats, onsite meetings, consulting / coaching, and media appearances.

When you call me, ask me how you can get 100 free books for your event! Visit marketingwithaheart.com/speaking

Cheers,

Ben

Chapter 3
PROFIT

While your message will change one life, your marketing can change thousands, if not millions of lives. You'll learn simple principles to communicate more persuasively, be more profitable, help more people, and inspire others through your message, work, and example.

¡Viva la Revolución!

SELLING IS SERVICE when you have the right intention and what you offer will help people.

Your offer is not just the price...

It's the relationship...the conversation...the influence and sales process...what you'll deliver...articulation of the results... and empathy with your audience...

It's acknowledging people's pain...reconnecting them with their desires...and supporting them with the logical and emotional elements of their decisions...

It's addressing all the concerns, objections and reasons that they may have for not investing in your product or service...

Then, when they've realized that they finally found someone to help them, when they know they can trust you...

...when they believe in your ability and in what you offer...

...when you've helped them understand the value and the results they'll get...that you're available to support them...when you've shared your "no risk" guarantee...

...then just imagine...

...what people will feel like, knowing they will finally be able to accomplish something they've been waiting for but haven't been able to (until you came along)...

...what a relief that is!

Selling is service when you (compassionately and ethically) take people through a process of influence in a way that supports them, and will change their lives.

¡Viva la Revolución!
Case Study

"SELLING IS SERVICE," I was sharing with Ethan, "and it's a two way street.

You need to serve yourself too.

"You're making a big impact, are committed, and work hard at it every day.

"So don't sell yourself short.

"You believe in your stuff and know that the value you are delivering is worth at least 10X your client's investment.

"When some people learn how much you charge, they may ask for a reduction.

"Consider it. But don't just reduce the price. Otherwise you are no longer a professional services provider, right?

"And people may undervalue what you offer.

"If it feels right, invite them to have a conversation with you.

"Make sure they are serious and committed to the results because you know you're over delivering on value already.

"Help them understand why the price is what it is.

"If they're really unable to afford it (and if it feels right), you can work out some kind of payment plan.

"But you don't have to make that a part of your main offer... just make it available to the people who really need it.

"Most of the time, don't reduce the price.

"Make the payment easier.
Or if you find you must reduce the price, then consider reducing what you deliver."

Inspiration Alone Will Leave You Broke and Bitter

REAL CHANGE, THE kind of transformation that becomes permanent, comes from two places:

1. inspiration; and

2. follow through.

Most people market and sell only inspiration, which is a disservice.

Buyers get hooked on the energy and emotion but can't sustain either for long enough to make real personal or professional transformation happen.

After inspiration comes the real work.

And that's when people need the most help.

This is why you want to offer a coaching or continuity/ membership program...to help people succeed and help your business thrive.

At a live event, speech, seminar, training, teleconference, webinar, or a Google Hangout, you have created a safe environment, where anything is possible.

But then people go back to life and business and need your help implementing the tools and strategies for success.

As someone who wants to make major positive impact, you want to deliver both inspiration and follow through: the best tools, strategies, and resources to show people what's possible (to create an immediate shift), as well as ongoing support (to create positive, permanent, transformation).

If you have something you know will change lives, it's your personal responsibility to make people aware of it (through marketing) and get them to take it home (through persuasion and selling).

Inspiration Alone Will Leave You Broke and Bitter

Case Study

JANELLE JUST PUBLISHED her first book.

After years as a corporate executive, she teaches women entrepreneurs the mindset, systems, and strategies that can benefit small businesses and solopreneurs.

We're clarifying the offer for her coaching program: why it's the right choice to work with her.

What we identify here will be used for her marketing, speeches, webinars, and enrollment calls.

These are the 7 core benefits of great coaching:

1. No great success happens alone, in business or life.

2. A great coach will listen, point you in the right direction, inspire and motivate you, and share his or her experiences.

3. Concert pianists, Olympic athletes, and successful business people all work with coaches.

4. Coaches can teach you (or go deeper into) the systems, strategies, and tactics from their speech, training, seminar, and/ or book.

5. Coaches pay for themselves by keeping you from reinventing the wheel (as well as avoiding mistakes)...so you can make money faster.

6. Coaches help you take the right action at the right time... with clarity, intention, and focus.

7. Coaches can connect you to the right people, are your best critics/reality check, and are there to celebrate your successes with you.

How To Take The Sleaze Out of Selling

LOTS OF PEOPLE think selling is sleazy.

There are many reasons: what we were taught growing up, media messages, and popular culture.

But it's the intention (your motivation) behind the action that's most important (just like everything in life).

If you are selling something just to get money and only benefit yourself, that's sleazy.
(Bad intention.)

But if you are selling something to help people make positive change in their lives, while providing yourself value, fulfillment, and the ability to help more people, then selling becomes service.

Imagine this...

How would you serve someone you care deeply about?

You would explain what you're offering.

You would share why you're doing it, what outcome you're hoping to help them achieve, and how it's going to happen.

You would help them understand if it's right for them and why.

Then you would invite them to join you by offering a genuine, heartfelt invitation.

Part of making the invitation is to let them know (with clarity and confidence), what kind of investment they should expect.

You want to help them understand the value of what you offer and that you're delivering results and outcomes that have already changed people's lives.

How To Take The Sleaze Out of Selling
Case Study

ARTHUR IS A wellness coach with a large email list, is selling products, and has a full coaching program (one-on-one).

He wants to offer group coaching:

1. so he can help more people; and

2. to free up time, since he's expecting his first child.

We discussed a strategy using webinars and Google Hangouts.

He would deliver high value content, then invite people into a private conversation.

(He wanted to ensure a good fit for himself, the client-to-be, and the group.)

He would also offer a 100% risk free 30 day money back satisfaction guarantee.

Arthur got more and more excited as we spoke.

Without any pitching or hard selling, he would be able to bring his curriculum to a full audience on each call, just by inviting people from his list.

Through the Q&A, he would learn (from his audience) how to refine his program and deliver even more value.

He would also be able to price his program lower than his individual coaching, and provide more access to him through a Facebook group. This would facilitate community support, interaction, and accountability.

And if our discussion wasn't exciting enough, Arthur realized that he could formalize his group coaching and license it to other coaches.

Weird? Help More People By Selling Them More Stuff

IF YOU HAVE a product or service that you know will change people's lives, it's important to realize that all of what you can offer to them (i.e. your knowledge, experience, skills, and expertise) can't be delivered in a single product, speech, or book.

It's part of your mission to make people aware and help them understand that they need more of your products and services, so they can get the full benefit of what you offer.

This is not about "getting people to buy more of your stuff".

This is about offering people the ongoing opportunity to have their lives impacted in a major way through everything that you offer.

It also gives you the opportunity to offer your products and services to different people in ways that fit their needs.

• Some people will benefit most from hearing you speak.

• Some from your video training.

• Others from reading your book.

• Certain people will get the most out of coaching, one-on-one with you.

• Some people will thrive in a group mastermind that you facilitate.

• Some people will benefit from a combination of all of these.

And this last group of people will probably be your best, longest term, most valuable clients.

Weird? Help More People By Selling Them More Stuff
Case Study

TINA KNEW SHE could serve more people and make more money by offering her expertise in a variety of ways.

But she didn't want to produce and market a lot of stuff without a plan. It didn't fit her personality and would be a big drain of time, energy, and money.

She knew, although plans change (and change again), that planning is key to success. And simple is better.

So I offered her some reflections for creating her plan, based on her core offer of group coaching.

1. "What kind of outcome/transformation will happen from being in the group. How will you message that?

2. "Who will benefit from, and value being in, the group?

3. "What is your offer and sales message?

4. "How will you enroll people? What do you need to do that?

5. "How will you promote the offer? What do you need to do that?

6. "How will you deliver the group coaching? What do you need to do that?

7. "What will you call the group?"

By starting here, we would be able to define her marketing and sales funnels, optimize her content creation, and choose the highest leverage actions that will bring her the fastest results.

The Guaranteed One Step Method To
Kill Your Business Fast

COMPETING ON PRICE is the guaranteed one step method to kill your business fast.

Consider that as an authority, expert, or professional services provider, you have done a lot to invest in your skills, abilities, confidence, and mastery.

You've likely studied and/or acquired experience for many years and invested tens or even hundreds of thousands of dollars in your success.

When you go to a specialist that you trust, you know that the cost isn't an issue if you have a big enough desire for the outcome you want.

Doctors, dentists, and other specialists charge a fortune, and for good reason.

People don't invest only based on price.

Other factors are results, trust, who they resonate with, and what they hear from other people.

So when you make an offer or quote a fee, educate people and give them the opportunity to really connect with you in order to understand the value of what you offer.

If you're providing real value that will change a person's life (and explaining it so they really understand it), then the main issue is no longer the price.

It's the cost (in time, money, energy, and emotional pain) of the person NOT taking action.

The Guaranteed One Step Method To
Kill Your Business Fast
Case Study

IN AN INDUSTRY that's saturated with "gurus" and charlatans, Gabe is the real deal.

Even with multiple degrees, 20 years of experience, and staying current in his field, he's not getting the steady stream of clients he's used to.

When we met, he considered reducing his rates.

I shared my thoughts:

"The best thing that you can do is show people how working with you is going to benefit them in a way that they have not considered yet.

"Part of that is helping them realize that you understand their challenges and why they might not be reaching their goals.

"Teach them that you will help them reach the outcomes they want, in a way that positions you differently from your competition.

"To make this work, you really have to know your audience and what they want so you can connect deeply with them. After 20 years, I know you do.

"And remember that people do funny things.

"Imagine doing a side by side comparison of two cars. All else appearing equal, one costs 25% more than the other.

"Wouldn't you assume that the more expensive car is better?

"It's not logical, but it's what most people do.

"So my friend, don't reduce your rates."

From No, No, No, No, No, No, To YES!

ADVERTISERS AND MARKETERS have discovered (and confirmed, over decades) that it usually takes 7-13 "touches" before someone will invest in what you offer, assuming that it's something that solves a problem they have.

So getting a person to invest in you is really about having an ongoing conversation with them.

Because, often, "no" means "not now".

The other challenge is how most of us were raised. The numbers may vary, but the nutshell is that for every 3 positives, we heard 25 negatives.

That means most of us heard the word "no" 40,000 times and the word "yes" only 5,000 times throughout childhood.

What this means to you is that most of your prospects are conditioned to say "no".

So there are psychological influence factors that you must use for your marketing, your selling, and your ability to change lives.

1. You want people to know you, like you, trust you and see you as a credible authority, especially through social proof (testimonials and case studies).

2. You want to cultivate a sense of commitment (by inviting people to take some kind of action) and reciprocity (by consistently delivering value) so people will respond favorably when you make a request or an offer.

3. You want to communicate scarcity (example: that there are only so many available slots and for a limited time).

You can (and should) use combinations of these factors, ethically, in all of your communications.

From No, No, No, No, No, No, To YES!
Case Study

VERONICA TEACHES WOMEN social entrepreneurs how to run their businesses profitably so they can focus on serving people.

Her business is growing through referrals.

But she recognizes the need to attract clients in other ways, and to serve them beyond one-on-one interactions.

We discussed her optin content (to grow her email list), low cost product (to see if people will buy), and core offer (group coaching plus VIP one-on-one coaching).

We analyzed her website and funnel (email autoresponder, optin pages, and sales pages).

To begin, we changed the tone of her language to be less formal and added a few videos to give people a sense of her as a person and how it would be to work with her.

Then we added more messages to her autoresponder (automatic emails that are sent when people subscribe to her list) for a total of 12.

This would create more of a "conversation" as well as consistency and top of mind awareness.

It would remind people that she could be counted on to follow through with what she promised.

We added case studies and video testimonials to her website and sales pages (for likability, trust, authority, and social proof).

Finally, we let people know about deadlines and limited space in Veronica's VIP coaching (scarcity).

When and Why You Want To Push People Over The Edge

THERE ARE SITUATIONS when you want people to make a choice right away, because hesitation can lead to indecision... which can lead to inaction...which leads nowhere near a sale.

There are other situations when people need time to make decisions.

And if you don't allow this, they feel pressured and you definitely lose the sale.

There needs to be balance.

You'll want to respect a person's need for time and space.

At the same time, you'll want to make sure to have a follow up conversation (within the week) so you don't lose the momentum.

Most people want to feel connected to other people at the point of making a decision, whether it's immediate or something that will take them longer.

If too much time passes, people will get stuck in their heads where the fear, doubt, and hesitation are (and you're not), and you won't be able to help them.

So, how will you best serve people, while ethically influencing them to take a leap that will transform their lives (all the while respecting their time and space and unique process)?

Here is where the serious magic happens, for both of you.

I invite you...to create the space.

When and Why You Want To Push People Over The Edge

Case Study

JANA HELPS PEOPLE transition from the corporate world into working from home.

She's been a one-woman show for years...everything from marketing to product creation to administration to bookkeeping.

She's known for a long time that she needs to fire herself from most of those jobs so she can focus on what she does best.

I recommended a company that offers a team of virtual employees with a project manager for a monthly fee.

She said that she needed time to consider it.

I supported her need for reflection and we made plans for breakfast at the end of the week.

As we sat down to coffee and croissants, I asked Jana if she'd made a decision.

She said she was still on the fence.

So I asked Jana to imagine two scenarios, one at a time.

First, how would life and business look if she continued exactly the same way?

How would she feel waking up each day?

What about 5 and 10 years from today?

Then I asked her to imagine what her business and life would look like, today, if she hired the team of virtual employees.

What about 5 and 10 years from today?

Her next choice became very clear.

So did the smile in her eyes.

How To Be The Belle of The Ball Even If You're A Guy

NETWORKING AND MARKETING have a common factor: people.

And when you bring authenticity, integrity, service, and heart into the conversation, the results are fantastic.

When you're networking (like marketing), you want people to know, like, and trust you...as well as understand that you can help them or someone they know.

Here's how you can make this happen.

During the conversation, listen deeply with your eyes, ears, heart, and head, and care about their response.

Make sure to keep facing them, stand up straight, and smile.

Be curious and ask questions.

People will like you simply because they are talking about themselves, and you are listening with empathy. Be sure to use the word "you" often. Say their name now and then as well.

Figure out how you can serve them first.

This allows you to begin every conversation from a place of service and creates the psychological trigger of reciprocity, which encourages the other person to want to help you.

Here are 5 ways you can serve: 1) offer an endorsement or a testimonial; 2) teach them something; 3) invest in their product or service; 4) give them "time" by helping out someone who they want to support; and 5) be their connection to other people.

By starting from a place of giving, you will get more of the right business, faster.

How To Be The Belle of The Ball Even If You're A Guy
Case Study

BILL, THE PRESIDENT of a division of an international university, was headed to an event with presidents from other schools and programs.

He knew that his online platform would revolutionize the learning environment for graduate students in biology. He was eager to serve his students and peers by creating alliances.

We chatted on Skype about his networking checklist.

We agreed that Bill would begin the conversation by making a personal connection and creating rapport, before moving onto any professional discussion.

Bill would then ask the other person about their professional role before speaking about himself.

We also recognized that the conversation needs to flow.

So we put the finishing touches on his *service-based* elevator pitch which emphasizes who he helps and the benefits that his online platform provides.

"I'm Bill with ([Name] International University)."

"I help grad students connect with other grad students worldwide: to collaborate, inspire each other, and cross pollinate ideas.

"This is good for the students and the faculty because of (X, Y, and Z).

"Do you know any division presidents whose students and faculty would benefit from this kind of collaborative learning environment?"

Lastly, we made sure that Bill didn't forget to ask, "How can I help you?"

The Power and Pitfalls of Telesummits

TELESUMMITS ARE POWERFUL, when you do them the right way.

By interviewing people in your niche (who complement you), you become an "expert" simply because you are the interviewer.

Telesummits also create exposure for the interviewees (as thought leaders) because each of them will be answering questions about their specific topic.

You can grow your email list since the people on your list will invite others they know.

The interviewees will also promote to their lists. Those folks will subscribe to your list because you are offering the interviews.

You can make sales.

You can create value by offering the live calls for free (and a replay for 24-48 hours).

Then you can sell a package of all the recordings for one price (before the event) and then at a higher price (during and after).

Some of the revenue will come from affiliates; many of the affiliates will be the folks you interview.

So if a person from (your affiliate) Mary's list invests in the recordings, you and Mary will split the sale, 50/50.

Additionally, when you are interviewing Mary and she offers her coaching package, sales that come from that offer will also be split 50/50.

It's a win-win-win: for you, Mary, and the person who invested.

The Power and Pitfalls of Telesummits
Case Study

YESTERDAY I GOT a call from a colleague who's been running her own telesummit. Things aren't going well.

She's getting very few optins and even fewer sales. We identified 3 key issues:

1) setting realistic marketing expectations;

2) partnering with the right speakers who have great products/services and big lists; and

3) making sure they promote as they promised.

I acknowledged her pain and honesty. She knows what to avoid in the future, but still needs to get through the telesummit today.

So I offered 3 suggestions.

1. "Don't let the speakers off the hook. Crack the whip and remind them of their commitment. This is your MAIN job right now. They've got to hear from you EVERY DAY.

2. "Consider running contests like "the most optins today gets a prize" so it's at least fun, and can give you a way to stimulate their competitive juices. This will create social proof that other speakers are truly committed and taking action.

3. "See who else can promote you, who you didn't already consider."

She plans to do another telesummit. She knows what to do better next time. Happily, she also knows that she hasn't failed. She's simply learned and grown.

My Cat Is Playing The Ukulele!

THERE ARE TWO ways to use social media.

The first is to broadcast things like, "Check out my cat! He's playing the ukulele!"

The second is to use it in a way that will serve your audience and grow your business.

If you're a thought leader, speaker, author, entrepreneur, or coach, content is key to positioning you as an authority on your topic, to keep your audience engaged, and for Google to like you.

So put most of your content on your blog and use social media to announce that it's there.

Drive traffic to your website and get people onto your email list.

If you release a 15-20 minute video, chances are you will have 2-5 major points.

Each Facebook post can discuss each point.

You can repeat and reword those posts 2-4 times in a day because most people only look at what's most recent in the Facebook stream. In addition, Facebook only shows each of your posts to a small portion of your audience.

You can also use social media to syndicate events (like a Google Hangout.)

You can publish the YouTube video (of the Hangout) on a Facebook tab (in real time) for the people who spend time on Facebook. At the same time you can post on Google+ for the folks in that audience.

And yes, if you want, you can still put up the picture of your cat. (Send me a message and I'll show you mine too!)

My Cat Is Playing The Ukulele!
Case Study

JAY IS A speaker who teaches people how to network. From his keynotes and trainings he has a wealth of content.

He knows he needs to use social media but doesn't want to deal with the potential time suck it can create.

When we started working together, Jay thought the best approach was to publish everything.

I recommended a more effective and saner approach.

"It's not as important to get a lot of content out there as it is to get good content in front of a lot of people.

"You can publish a piece of content once each week and spend the rest of the week promoting it.

"This is easy to outsource.

"Take your 20 minute video and carve it into five segments to make a series of posts.

"Outsourcers can transcribe the video, create teasers, post articles, post to your blog, and create podcasts.

"You can put each video on your YouTube channel, blog, and Facebook.

"You can use Facebook advertising to drive people to a tab on your page.

"No matter where you drive the traffic, be sure to use a call to action...to create social proof and engagement or to get people onto your list."

[Reminder: did you get the training and framework from page 1? If not, visit marketingwithaheart.com/bookgift]

When Keyword Research Is A Big Fat Waste of Time

IF YOUR IDEAL customer or client is the person you can help the most (and the right person to buy your stuff)...and you understand that you must know a lot about this person (as well as their psychological drivers so you can do good marketing)...

...then can you honestly say that you really know who your customer or client is?

If you're not completely sure, what does that mean for your marketing, list building, and sales?

You can spend a lot of time trying to precisely identify who your audience is from indirect research: keywords, trends, insights, etc.

But that's like being in the laboratory while your audience is out in the world.

Instead, start with what you know.

Put something out there, drive traffic, and see if you get comments, shares, feedback, or anything else that gives you a better idea of who the audience really is and what they are interested in.

Then you can do your research more effectively.

Additionally, ask a lot of questions, do surveys, and offer free 15 minute coaching calls (where you help people and pay close attention to see what keeps coming up).

That's the most reliable way I've found, because it allows me to engage with people, find out more about them, identify trends in motivation and language, and serve them directly.

And it's more fun!

When Keyword Research Is A Big Fat Waste of Time Case Study

VIVIAN HAD AN idea for a new product.

She started sketching out what she thought was her ideal customer, and was ready to jump into keyword research.

I recommended an alternate first step...not to replace keyword research but to make it more effective and likely deliver a few other benefits as well.

"Look at your niche and identify who your competition could be.

"Get on their emails lists, analyze their marketing and sales funnels, study their optin and sales pages, and invest in the $97-$197 product(s) that seem closest to what you'll offer.

"You'll have an accurate sense of the marketing and sales language that works (i.e. fears/frustrations/needs/desires/hopes), keywords to analyze, and the kinds of products that people are buying.

"After that, figure out which businesses could complement you, or that you could partner with.

"Follow the same process that I've already described, but instead look to see what you could offer them or how you can help them improve a product or service.

"It's easier and more time/energy/cost effective to see what's working in the marketplace, and then make your next moves based on what you know is successful."

The Right Time For Autopilot…and Not

SELLING YOUR SERVICES and enrolling people in your programs is ultimately based on the trust and confidence that people have in you.

The monthly investment for your services plus the relationship you've already built will generally indicate whether you need to have an enrollment call, and what kind.

Because people want to know and like you.

They need to see how good you are, understand that you "get them", and trust that you can deliver the transformation they want.

The more of this that happens (and is done well) beforehand will make the enrollment process easier.

As of this writing, asking people for $297 or less each month can often be done without an enrollment call.

Up to $497 a month usually needs a webinar, Hangout or group strategy/enrollment call so there's some personal contact with you.

When you go over $500 each month, you'll probably want to have a personal conversation…not just for getting someone in the door, but because they will most likely stay with you for longer.

In general, the more groundwork that has been laid (in terms of value, authority, and branding), and the lower the monthly investment, the more automated your enrollment process can be.

Remember, check out what's happening in your industry, and connect the price of your offer to the results you will deliver.

The Right Time For Autopilot...and Not
Case Study

DAVID IS AN author who teaches universal spiritual principles that people can use in life and in business.

He's been developing products and a coaching program.

He is clear on his pricing, but needed help clarifying enrollment calls...so he could minimize his time investment and maximize his sales.

Since his sales funnel is converting well, and after analyzing data from a recent launch, he knows that his $97 and and $197 products will sell without any kind of call or webinar...especially since he consistently delivers a ton of value and has cultivated a sizable, engaged email list.

From analyzing a series of his one-on-one enrollment calls and then a recorded webinar, we discovered that David could run an automated (evergreen) webinar to enroll people in his group coaching for $347/month.

While his conversions would be lower (since it's not live), it will free up his time and be selling 24/7.

For his $797 (monthly) one-on-one coaching, David will do a live teleseminar so he can talk to several people at once (for greater leverage).

From there he'll invite people to a one-on-one enrollment call.

He knows his conversions will be high because he offers even more value on these calls, and most people like him right away.

The 90 Day Business Builder and

Authority Machine™

The Solution For Entrepreneurs, Small Businesses, and Organizations Who Are Making A Positive Impact In The World

Do you want to build your business or enter a new, profitable market in just 90 days?

1. We help you create your entire sales funnel.
2. We build your online authority through content and video.
3. We drive targeted traffic (via advertising) to your site.

Results

People subscribe to your list. You develop a relationship and give them lots of value. They invest in your products, services, and / or programs. **You transform their lives.**

How It Works

1. Driving Targeted Traffic To Your Site

   Then The Right People Subscribe To Your List

2. Creating Your Sales Funnel

   So People Choose To Invest In What You Offer

[We provide frameworks, consulting and 2 rounds of edits for all the content. We also offer done-for-you options if you prefer that we create it for you (with your input, of course). This is a great way to save yourself hours of time and the headache of creating all this content.]

Visit marketingwithaheart.com/90daybusiness

Chapter 4

PRINCIPLES

Principles are the foundation of Marketing With A Heart™ and are the bedrock for People, Purpose, and Profit. You'll discover perspectives and insights about your journey to success, service, being happy, and creating the business and life you want. You'll also learn what makes a business truly sustainable, more profitable, and impactful.

Marketing Is A Love Affair

MOST MARKETING CAMPAIGNS don't work.

Beware of coaches, consultants, and gurus who claim otherwise because they are marketing and selling to you, unethically.

That's why you want to get things out there as quickly as possible, so you can get feedback from your audience that will inform your next steps.

When you begin any marketing campaign you want to go in with as little attachment to the outcome as possible.

Or put another way, expect the best but be flexible and ready for the worst.

(This is good business.)

You want to be inspired, take some risks, and committed to getting your ideas out there fast, while at the same time be ready to let them go if they don't work.

If it's not resonating with your audience, you can ask them questions, understand their experience, see what you can do better, and then offer something else.

Like love affairs, most marketing campaigns don't work.

But for those that do, imagine the kinds of transformation you will create, in your life and for the people you serve!

Don't ever stop marketing with a heart and don't ever give up on love.

There are people who need your message and are waiting for you right now.

Marketing Is A Love Affair
Case Study

I WAS RECENTLY chatting with the host of an event. When we finished, she invited me onstage.

(It was the shortest speech I've given.)

"Marketing is a love affair. It's about giving your all while living without expectations.

"Imagine this...

"You feel that spark...that mysterious, magical, creative, loving force that comes out of nowhere and is suddenly everywhere...when you wake up...as you fall asleep, when you're eating...everywhere all the time.

"It's that brilliant idea that comes from inside you. The idea that's going to change people's lives because it's already changed yours. You can't wait to share it.

"Everything seems shiny and yummy and even the commuter traffic isn't so bad.

"But then, as you begin your marketing, you start to see what's not so shiny and yummy.

"Some people read your blog and leave a few comments. Fewer optin for your webinar. Even fewer show up.

"Nobody invests in your product. Your coaching program is still just an outline...

"Now you have two choices:

"You can give up (which is a true failure).

"Or...

"You can create the space for love and inspiration to fill your soul, transform your life, and give you another chance to change people's lives."

Failure Is The Fastest Road To Success

TRYING TO BE perfect is the fastest way to kill your business, your momentum, and your happiness. Notice I did not use the word "fail".

That's a concept that you'll want to redefine for yourself... because "failure" is simply information that helps you modify the direction you're going, so you can succeed faster.

Thomas Edison "failed" more than 1,000 times before he got the lightbulb to work.

The only two true "failures" are:

1. giving up; and
2. not getting started in the first place.

But for now, I want to talk about perfectionism...and how it has nothing to do with reaching your goals and achieving your dreams. You CANNOT be perfect AND be successful because you will never get anything done.

And success in business, especially marketing, relies on doing things fast.

Take my word for it.

Or better yet, test this out yourself.

The sooner you get a blog post, video, proposal, or offer in front of your audience, the sooner you'll get feedback that you've hit the mark...or need to go back to the drawing board... or somewhere in between.

Now that I think about it, there is actually a third true "failure".

It's called perfectionism.

Failure Is The Fastest Road To Success
Case Study

ANTON IS AN environmental lawyer who is moving into the speaking arena.

He's also a recovering perfectionist.

We're developing his sales funnel: taking people from his free optin content (a.k.a. lead magnet), to his low cost product (a.k.a. tripwire), to his core offer...which is a group coaching program.

It all starts with content creation. Anton wants it all to be perfect. I counter with some tough love instead.

"I want to invite you to make "good enough" your mantra. I can see that you're squirming when you hear me say that.

"So breathe...

"When you apply this mantra to your content creation, the outcomes will be tremendous.

"Because there's no guarantee your marketing will work (contrary to what most marketing coaches, consultants, and gurus claim).

"You don't know what your audience will respond to. So the faster you get your stuff out there, the faster you'll get feedback (which is trackable, measurable, actionable data).

"Then you'll know to keep doing what's working and scrapping what's not.

"Your audience has the truth. Ask them for it. Let them guide you to offering them the products and services they truly want...not what you think they need.

"Then help them change their lives."

It's Not What You Say Or What You Do…

AS YOU LOOK back at the journey you took to get here…to see where you've been and where you are in relation to your life goals…it will be clear that you couldn't (and wouldn't) have gotten here without coming the way you came.

There aren't any other ways to go and there aren't any shortcuts.

You can't reach your goals without a few bumps, bruises, detours, and a lot of laughter along the way.

Everything has happened to teach you everything you need to know right now, to take the next step on your journey.

And one of the ongoing teachings is about self mastery and self discipline.

These are the tools that will help you get up (and keep getting up) after you get knocked down.

(Because, as you know, you will get knocked down a lot.)

Self mastery and self discipline are also the keys to your business success.

They are what clarify and fortify your authenticity, integrity, and character.

Because if you're being inauthentic, operating without integrity, or weak in your character, every relationship, communication, or marketing effort will fail, sooner or later.

People will eventually see through what's superficial.

Because it's ultimately not what you say or do…it's who you are and what you think.

It's Not What You Say Or What You Do…
Case Study

WHEN I THINK more about self discipline and self mastery, I think about how I am relating: to myself and to other people.

So I need to cultivate and care for these relationships.

It starts with commitment (to myself and others), in terms of a lifelong vision as well as a reminder every single day.

Today and everyday…

• I am committed to creating the best day of my life.

• I am committed to becoming the person I need to be through personal and spiritual development.

• I am committed to doing what's right (instead of what's easy) and consistently taking action. I can't wait…because now is my time, and I don't know how long (or short) my life will be.

• I am committed to the success and fulfillment that I am truly capable of and deserve, because it will benefit myself and everyone I touch.

• I am committed to success that's based on truth and integrity, so my thoughts, words, and actions will benefit all beings.

• I am committed to smiling, laughing, and giving myself a break.

• I am committed to being perfectly human.

I know I will make mistakes. When I do, I will accept responsibility, learn what I need, and move on.

All The Ways Life Taught You To Be Unsuccessful

DID YOU EVER pause to think about all of the learning in your life?

There's what we learned at school and what we learned from our parents and friends.

What (many of us) learned from television.

There's what the internet teaches. What work teaches. What debt teaches. What our mistakes teach.

What philosophy, religion, and spirituality teach. What altered states of consciousness teach.

What our spouses or partners teach. What our children teach. What our pets teach. What sickness, old age, and death teach.

That's a lot of teaching, from when we were young and very impressionable...to where we are now and (hopefully) less impressionable (and a bit wiser and more discerning).

So based on that, what does it mean to be a lifelong learner?

For many people, it's a matter of acquiring more knowledge and information for personal and/or professional reasons.

But that's not the whole story.

For as much as we need to keep learning and understanding, there's as much, if not more, that we need to unlearn and release, so we can grow.

Otherwise success is limited by the roles, stories, and beliefs that have been handed to us, rather than what we've discovered for ourselves.

All The Ways Life Taught You To Be Unsuccessful Case Study

REGINA AND I were discussing how much of what she learned in her life was creating a ceiling on her success: in her business and personal life.

She was ready to let go and break through.

The first was "being the best".

She'd attended a top academic university.

Although there was a lot of lip service to "doing your best is what's important", in reality there was no such thing as second place.

So Regina redefined excellence for herself in a way that felt more supportive.

The second was the idea that the path of business has to be along a straight line.

As a new entrepreneur, she was finally feeling ok with the fact that doors were opening in areas that she never envisioned.

Regina gave herself permission to make a shift in the business paradigm she'd been locked into, which helped her reach her goals faster.

Finally, Regina learned that she didn't have to do it all herself.

She could do what she loved while hiring and partnering with others to handle various aspects of the business.

She recognized that she needed to have enough general knowledge of "the other stuff" so she could be an effective leader and strategist.

Thinking, Speaking, Feeling and Expecting It To Be Real

FOR THOUSANDS OF years, among science, religion, spirituality, metaphysics, personal development, psychology, athletics, and more, there has been (and is) the understanding that what we think and say creates our reality.

21st century scientists, athletes, and high performers prove this fact. What happens in the brain (neurologically) and the body (chemically) when we do something...is the same as when we think about doing that same thing.

That's why so many athletes, high performers, and other people dedicate time and energy to envisioning and affirming success. Whether it's winning a gold medal, public speaking, self healing, or just relaxing, the power of affirmations and visualization is astounding. Fortunately, the methods are simple and available to everyone.

They need to happen regularly (become a habit) and be done the right way.

Affirmations should be in the present tense, have an emotional component, include "I", be specific and tangible, and said in the positive ("I am wealthy" vs. "I don't have debt").

As you visualize, picture your successful outcomes as if you have achieved them already.

Take a moment now.

Think about a goal or dream of yours.

What do you see? Hear? Feel? Taste? Smell?

Use your imagination...and use your six senses.

What are you experiencing/feeling/seeing/smelling/hearing/ touching as you realize your dream has come true?

Thinking, Speaking, Feeling and
Expecting It To Be Real
Case Study

DWAN IS A financial coach who wants to integrate affirmations and visualization into his work with clients.

Although he uses them both regularly, he wasn't sure how his clients would receive them.

I reminded Dwan that every communication is, in essence, a marketing campaign.

It's key to remember who the audience is, so you can speak to them in their language, about things they find important. Then connect the dots for them.

I suggested that he emphasize the fact that the affirmation and visualization process is supported by science and is utilized by many athletes.

From there, he could guide his clients to capture their specific goals by writing them down, saying them out loud, and telling people (since public declarations are incredibly powerful).

Over time, he could suggest that his clients create vision boards, but perhaps call them "success and goals boards".

I offered a real life analogy.

An actor named Eric Garcetti worked on the TV cop show "The Closer" and its spin-off series "Major Crimes" from 2010 to 2012.

He played the mayor of Los Angeles.

In 2013, in real life, he ran for mayor of L.A. and won.

Tell Your Inner Critic To Shut The Heck Up

DO YOU HAVE that critical, inner voice that sometimes whispers, "people will say, 'You're not that good after all!'"

When I hear that, I take a big, deep breath and say, "Whoa, that's not true! That's just mind chatter. And if everybody isn't happy, so what?"

Ultimately I have to reframe it, consistently reframe when I hear that voice...to remind myself that this journey isn't just about me.

This is about trying to help as many people as I can by sharing my message.

And some will appreciate it, some won't.

Some folks have nothing better to do than criticize others, especially those of us who make their dreams come true. That's how they validate themselves.

I remind myself of this because sometimes my inner voice seems to take sides with these people.

Additionally, if I compare myself to people I admire, then I could easily spend a whole day talking myself right out of business.

So it's a conscious effort to reframe that intimidation into inspiration.

I know that if I were to speak to these people, they would support and encourage me.

(Because I have. And they do.)

They are not better than me.

They're a little further down the road AND they have the same kinds fears and doubts and mind chatter to deal with.

Tell Your Inner Critic To Shut The Heck Up
Case Study

MARGIE IS ABOUT to do her first launch.

She has an amazing offer, a responsive email list, a proven sales funnel, and several affiliates who will be promoting for her.

As the big day approaches, her biggest problem is that she's not sleeping so well.

As a VIP, inner circle client of mine, she's able to call or text me when she needs (within reason, of course).

I've had a few quick discussions with her recently, about the chatter in her head.

I reminded her that it's part of how our brains work, to keep us safe.

It's also the ego trying to maintain the status quo when it feels threatened by change.

The inner critic isn't who she is.

The words aren't true although they may feel true right now.

And the best thing is to get them out of her system, out of her muscle memory, and out of her consciousness.

Some tools that Margie knows work well are journaling, affirmations, dancing, meditating, and massage.

No matter the tool, the goal is to be present, more focused, feel in control, and accomplish the outcome(s).

This is training herself to believe that when she wants to do something, she can.

Regardless of that little voice.

The Road To Success Is Like
Driving Along Godzilla's Highway

THE ROAD TO success is an ongoing journey that's paved with potholes.

And that's the beauty.

There is no such thing as perfect success.

And that's what makes it real and available to you (and me).

Because success is a journey, it's not just in the future, "someday". Success is actually achieved each day, often many times in a day, in large and small ways.

You just need the right perspective and attitude.

You have a unique mix of passion, vision, and talent. There has never been, nor will there ever be, another you.

So right now is your opportunity and challenge to be successful today...and in a future that's far more amazing than anything you can imagine right now.

Success gives powerful tests: "losing", "failure", "embarrassment", "doubt", perfectionism, "fear", and "procrastination".

Passing these tests is success...and they never stop.

The more you discover yourself, your power, and who you truly are, the more success, wealth, and abundance you will create.

At the same time, you will have more responsibility to yourself and to the world around you.

This is the price of success.

In my opinion, it's well worth it.

The Road To Success Is Like
Driving Along Godzilla's Highway
Case Study

RORY IS SOMEONE you may recognize.

Like me, he's a recovering perfectionist.

And that's one of the many aspects that make it a delight to be working together.

From our weekly calls, Rory was able to tap into something huge. He realized that his perfectionism was his comfort zone.

And as you know, it's only outside of your comfort zone that true magic happens. Rory knew this too, but was terrified.

So we devised ways that he could step out of his comfort zone, but at an acceptable 10% (according to his standards).

As Rory began his 10% paradigm shift, he felt shaky and had to rely on lots of deep breathing and a few extra coaching calls.

But he recognized that the doors of opportunity were beginning to open...because he was now taking risks and empowering himself.

The right people and the right resources started showing up, even as he lost some clients and faced some financial setbacks.

And because Rory had a flexible plan, his opportunities for success skyrocketed, even during the chaotic times.

Since his vision aligned with his principles (in serving others) and now that other people could clearly see it, Rory created a client and affiliate base much greater than he'd ever imagined.

He took a risk that brought him incredible rewards.

The Compassionate Ass Kicking

WHETHER YOU'RE STARTING a new business or doing something new in your current business, one of the biggest challenges you'll face is taking that first step.

It's about saying yes to your vision every day.

Getting started is literally about getting started.

You don't have to get it right. Just get it going.

This is where the phrase "imperfect action beats perfect inaction" comes into play.

Some people think they need "THE PLAN".

But the plan is simply the tool that will get you started.

You might feel fear. (We all do.) Do it anyway.

Fear is a physical expression of how much you care about making your vision into a reality.

Here are 5 ways to say yes to your vision, each day:

1. Every morning, remind yourself what it is, who you're serving, and why you're doing it.

2. Create deadlines (due dates and lengths of time). Put them on the calendar.

3. Get an accountability partner and speak at least five mornings each week.

4. Broadcast to your entire network when you will accomplish a goal so you can create external motivation and stay true to your word.

5. Get a coach so you can get whatever's blocking you out of the way.

The Compassionate Ass Kicking
Case Study

WHEN I FIRST met Antonia, she was stuck.

She'd been working with a business partner for the last 10 years and knew it was time to end the relationship and start her own business.

Antonia coaches people to higher levels of personal and professional success.

Like most of us, Antonia couldn't look at her own situation with the same clarity and objectivity that she offered to others.

I was afraid that her challenges (around starting her own business) would contaminate the coaching space with her clients...and therefore she wouldn't serve them in the best way possible.

I shared my perspective: that her worries about money and time, as well as her tendency to be overly forgiving toward herself, (read: indulgent) would jeopardize her ability to serve her clients as her highest, best, most courageous self.

If she wasn't addressing her concerns (which were keeping her from taking action) and being too self indulgent (by not giving herself a compassionate ass-kicking)...then asking her clients to step up would be hypocritical.

Coaches must lead by example.

Otherwise, their advice can come across as hollow and will lack the power that would otherwise help people break through the challenges that are holding them back.

Forget Would've, Could've, Should've, and If Only

ONE WISE PERSON (at least) has offered this advice: "obsessing on the past means living in a state of regret. Obsessing on the future means living in a state of worry."

Welcome to this moment. Every thought, word, and action that you've created, spoken, and taken has brought you to right now.

It can be very seductive to look back to "better days". Depending on the situation now, some time in the past may have been better.

Or not.

We all have the ability to reframe and re-create the past into something much less painful or much more amazing than it actually was. It's equally seductive to look to the future.

"*When* I get a raise..."

"*When* I lose weight..."

"*When* I'm healthy..."

"*When* I have a partner..."

"*When* I'm single..."

"*When* the government stops taking all my money..."

One wise person (at least) has also shared, "the past is history, the future is a mystery, the present is a gift...that's why it's called the present."

Can you honor and learn from your past, while being present with your life and experiencing today...so you can create a future that's more amazing than you can imagine?

(I know you can.)

Forget Would've, Could've, Should've, and If Only

Case Study

BENJAMIN FRANKLIN (a man with a fabulous first name) once stated, "in this world nothing can be said to be certain, except death and taxes".

I'd like to add one more: change. It's happening all the time.

Yet we are conditioned to think things are permanent...while in reality everything that arises is going to pass away.

That means people, animals, thoughts, emotions, feelings, perspectives, fashion trends, bad weather, fad diets, good weather, grudges, infatuations...everything.

When you get down to it, on an atomic and subatomic level, matter is changing trillions of times each second. Because everything is fundamentally energy, including your thoughts.

That means you and everything you are/think/feel/experience is changing...trillions of times each second...even though things seem be solid/lasting/permanent.

So what can you do with that? I remind myself:

1. to tell people how much I love and care for them (often) because we're all going to die...and we don't know when or how...

2. that no matter how much things "suck", this too will pass...

3. that no matter how wonderful things are, this too will pass...

4. that I'm never actually stuck in who I "think" I am, and there is opportunity for radical transformation, literally each second...

Stop Freaking Out Because You Can't Do It All Anyway

IF YOU TRY to feel competent by anticipating everything you need to master you'll probably feel incompetent. Because there's a lot that you want to do and accomplish. And there all of the things that you're used to achieving.

And now you realize you're starting again. You're a beginning learner again.

That can create a big information gap and a lot of anxiety as a result.

So I offer you the possibility to work it backwards.

Get your big vision in place. Then work it back to what you can do right now, so you really feel confident you're going to get that one thing done.

You know you need this one piece done, so you focus on it.

And when you get it done that's a piece of the puzzle...even if you not sure what the whole puzzle is right now.

Because when you get to the next piece, you know you've gotten the first piece handled, so you don't have to worry about it anymore.

And this next piece will make you have to focus and learn again.

But then, you'll have two pieces handled.

In a nutshell, you are are always focusing on learning one small thing at a time and then reinforcing that success.

So stop freaking out.

Just do the next thing and keep your vision on the big picture.

You'll get there.

Stop Freaking Out Because You Can't Do It All Anyway
Case Study

DEIRDRE RUNS 3 businesses, takes care of her parents, and has 4 dogs (two of whom are puppies).

On our calls, she lists everything she's learned and accomplished in the previous two weeks.

It's amazing and inspiring.

But to hear her talk about it…she's always worrying about how long things are taking.

Instead of focusing on where she is now (her successes) and where she wants to be (her vision), she often focuses on the gap in between.

Lots of "should have", "not enough", etc.

So part of my role is to reflect her accomplishments and reframe her challenges.

The other part is to help her shift her perspective.

A helpful tool to shift perspective is affirmations.

So Deirdre and I created one together that honors her current successes and her unremitting desire for excellence (for herself and so she can help other people).

"I am doing the best I can in this moment, and what I have already achieved today is helping many people.

"At the same time, I can and will do better so I can help even more people and accomplish what I am on this Earth to do."

Attitudes Are More Powerful Than Actions

WATCH OUT!

How you react to a problem might make the problem worse, last longer, or both. This is especially important with money.

When money is tight, a natural reaction might be to cut back. And whether you recognize it or not, your attitude may suddenly shift to lack and scarcity.

Here's where you'll want to be extremely careful.

The attitudes that you have about money (success, self-worth, love, and happiness for that matter) are much more powerful than the actions you take.

Your attitude precedes everything in your life.

Let me say that differently. Your attitude doesn't just affect your reality, it actually creates your reality: wealth, love, happiness, success, joy, and fulfillment.

Yes, it can be good to reduce costs. Of course.

But you want to avoid an attitude of lack and scarcity because you will imprint those messages on your subconscious.

The money (and love, joy, fulfillment, etc.) in your life is created by having a generous state of mind, regardless of the circumstances around you (which will change).

It's all about the imprints that you continue to plant in your subconscious, imprints that you strengthen or weaken every single day.

Every single moment.

Imprints that become the life around you.

So stay generous, even as you reduce costs.

Attitudes Are More Powerful Than Actions
Case Study

THE ATTITUDES YOU choose will make impressions on your subconscious and this, over time, will create your reality.

This is a truth that has come to us through thousands of years of wisdom and many spiritual traditions. It also comes to us from quantum physics.

In other words, your subconscious mind affects the people and the world around you. So choose your attitudes wisely.

The foundation of the universe is energy, and this energy is love.

(You can call it whatever or whomever you want, of course. I'm not here to tell you what or how to believe. I just want to share what works for me, contributes to my happiness, and gives me the opportunity to serve others in the most impactful way.)

So I do my best to choose attitudes that create a generous state of mind, so I can prosper in my business and in my life.

I do my best to live ethically to create a happy world.

I do my best to stay physically and mentally healthy, by minimizing my experiences of anger, worry, scarcity, doubt, and fear...so I can attract the people and situations that I want.

By taking joy in service, I cultivate my ability to lead by example.

Through meditation, I strengthen my capacity for compassion and wisdom, especially for when things get difficult.

And when I screw up, I take responsibility, take a deep breath, and take the next step toward my goals and dreams.

Will You Do Something For Me?

Write A Quick Book Review

If you're enjoying this book, will you please write a review? **Visit marketingwithaheart.com/review**

Here are a few questions to get you thinking...

1. What value did you receive?

2. How are you better off...in your business and/or in your life?

3. What message will use tomorrow?

4. How will you use what you've read to to increase your profits and help more people?

5. Why did you like (or dislike) this book?

6. What else would you like to know that I didn't cover in the book?

7. What new ideas did it generate?

8. What was your biggest surprise?

9. How is *Marketing With A Heart* different from other books you have read?

10. Is the content applicable to your business?

11. What type of person would most benefit from reading this book and working with me? Is there a particular person that comes to mind?

12. Is this book relevant to any particular industries?

13. What would you say to someone who is skeptical or on the fence about purchasing the book or working with me?

Afterword: The 5th "P" of
Marketing With A Heart...Possibility

IF YOU'RE AN executive, entrepreneur, politician, speaker, author, coach, trainer, consultant, or other purpose driven leader...you have an amazing opportunity.

When you listen to your audience's stories (whether it's a group, client, customer, colleague, partner, vendor, or other stakeholder) you get to know them and understand them deeply: their challenges, desires, what they can't stand, and what they care about most.

At the same time, when you tell your stories, they have a chance to experience the real, authentic you.

So when you communicate with them, amazing things happen...

You become a greater influencer.

You inspire people to greater action.

You become a greater leader (whether you're helping one person or impacting millions).

Conscious leaders, like you, can inspire and impact people in a way that elevates themselves and others.

You have this powerful tool of inspiration...conscious marketing.

You have this amazing opportunity to transform lives.

You can inspire people to be their best, and beyond.

You can continue helping people live happier, peaceful, more productive lives...many years after you and I have left this Earth.

This can be your legacy.

This is Possibility.

This is Marketing With A Heart™

Acknowledgments

IT'S A HUMBLING, fabulous experience when you think about how many beings support your life and your success...

From the most pivotal people to the person who delivered pizza when I was putting the finishing touches on this book...

I am so thankful every single day. The following acknowledgements barely scratch the surface of my gratitude. I know that there are people and animals who aren't mentioned here. Please know that you are in my heart, every day.

To the Earth: for food, water, air, magnificent nature, and gravity (so we don't go flying off into space)...

To my parents Irene & Pat Sheehy and Hilppa & Gerry Gioia. Thank you for birthing me, helping me grow, teaching me love and kindness, and always supporting my journey...

To my coaches and mentors, without whom this book (and my entire business) would never have happened: Lou D'Alo, James Malinchak, George Schofield...

To everyone in the PowerUp Coaching Gym and the Awesomesauce Mastermind...with a shout out to Dane Treat, Sara Pearl, Aleem Nasser, Jill Weadick, Christopher Browning, Shannon Cole, Barbara Rosson, Jesse Ali...

To all the beings who have supported my spiritual and human growth and development: Gautama Buddha, S.N. Goenka, Daphne Carvela, Eric Poche, Roy Remer, The Dalai Lama, Adyashanti, B. Alan Wallace, Layne Whitley, Grandmother Ayahuasca, Dave Stone, Nelson Mandela, Dr. Gabrielle Francis, Staja Hobsbawn, Russell Collins, Sally Northcutt, Alan Dysart, Elize Van Den Heever, Siddheshwari, Sri Nisargadatta Maharaj, Susana and Shimshai Cook, Malcolm X, Mary Morrissey, Bob

Proctor, everyone who entered the Zen Hospice Project Guest House with their breath (and then left the House without it)…

To all the people who have impacted my life as an entrepreneur: Eben Pagan, Brendon Burchard, Ken McArthur, Tracy Repchuk, Jim Rohn, Brian Tracy, Chris Widener, Davy Tybursky, LaVonna Roth, Annette Segal, Joy & Kellan Fluckiger, Cynthia Noonan, Erik Nelson, Sara Lahey, Linda de Mello, John Trauth, Donna "The Fairy Godmother" McCallum, Ken Christian, Michelle Garrison, Jeff Marcous, Yebuny Johnson, Margaret Ryan, Kim Brittingham, Mike Wolf, Debbie Peck, Nancy Ferrari…

To all my friends and every single member of my family (blood and otherwise) who have supported me with love, shelter, and (sometimes) cash as I took my dream and made it into reality: Nikki Stephens, Laura Branagan, Zeke Kossover, Linda Branagan, John Sweet, Nathan Walker, Lin Chase, Kathy McLaughlin, Grace & Sal Curcio, Steve Perzan, Sarah & Avrami Hendlish, Annie Schellenberg, Almendra Garcia, Constina & Eamon Howley…

To all the animals who I've been blessed to share some time with: Quito, Gozzi, Heru, Osiris, Owly, Tiger, Stallone, Oscar, Bear, CoCo, Milou, Mocha, Snoopy, Mojo, YoYo, Spirit, Jackson, Bella…

To everyone who helped produce this book: Cathy Presland (strategy), Donna Zucker (editing), Haisam Hussein (graphics), Leon Saperstein (cover photo) Johan del Barrio (design), Intel for the excellent font Clear Sans, Christian Robertson for the excellent font, Roboto, and Amazon.com.

Finally, to all the uncountable others who just magically appeared in my life and supported me in ways they probably don't even know. To each of you I offer so much love, gratitude, and a deep bow…Namaste.

Index

80/20 Rule | 42, 43

A

AARP | 13, 21
accountability | 71,93
ALS Association, The | 13, 21
affirmations | 69, 122, 123, 125, 133
attitude | 23, 26, 27, 71, 126, 134, 135
audience | 15, 16, 19, 29, 32, 35, 36, 37, 39, 40, 44, 45, 46, 48,
    51, 53, 67, 76, 82, 83, 85, 88, 93, 106, 108, 112, 114, 116,
    117, 123, 137
authentic, authenticity | 12, 14, 32, 33 102, 118
author | 1, 11, 12, 18, 29, 32, 33, 36, 37, 106, 111, 137
authority | 1, 12, 36, 37, 44, 47, 50, 60, 62, 68, 96, 98, 99, 106,
    110

B

bottom line | 12, 17, 25, 29, 30

C

coach, coaching | 11, 18, 23, 29, 32, 35, 37, 39, 40, 42, 43, 47,
    50, 53, 65, 67, 70, 71, 73, 75, 90, 91, 93, 94, 95, 99, 104, 106,
    108, 111, 114, 115, 117, 123, 127, 128, 129, 137
communication | 12, 26, 38, 39, 70, 146, 153
community | 23, 27, 93
compassion | 28, 32, 45, 50, 68, 88, 128, 129, 135
Condé Nast | 13, 21
conscious leadership | 13, 35, 78, 137
conscious marketing | 12, 13, 15, 17, 23, 30, 32-34
content | 1, 33, 39, 46, 47, 50, 51, 53, 93, 95, 99, 106, 107, 117

D

deadlines | 52, 99, 128
discipline | 29, 118, 119

E

empathize, empathy | 20, 23, 28, 35, 36, 37, 45, 88, 102

energy | 1, 11, 28, 29, 38, 40, 42, 44, 46, 48, 50, 53, 55, 67, 72, 74, 77, 78, 83, 84, 90, 95, 96, 109, 122, 131, 135

entrepreneur | 13, 18, 29, 32, 34, 37, 56, 61, 75, 91, 99, 106, 121, 137

F

failure | 17, 65, 115, 116, 117, 126

fear | 14, 30, 35, 36, 44, 46, 55, 56, 57, 109, 124, 126, 128, 135

freedom | 21, 30, 66

fulfillment, fulfilled | 12, 17, 19, 25, 30, 33, 63, 66, 69, 76, 86, 92, 119, 134

G

getting started | 116, 128

gift for you | 1

goals | 23, 32, 35, 42, 64, 68, 75, 84, 85, 97, 116, 118, 121, 123, 135

H

happiness, happy | 20, 21, 23, 25, 27, 45, 55, 66, 74, 82, 116, 124, 134, 135

Hearst | 13, 21

heart | (*"It's the entire book!"*)

I

impact | 11, 13, 14, 16, 19, 20, 22, 27, 29, 30, 32, 38, 43, 55, 58, 62, 64, 65, 69, 74, 86, 89, 90, 94, 112, 135, 136

income | 11, 13, 16, 19, 30, 32, 58, 75, 86, 112

India | 13, 21, 22

influence | 11, 13, 14, 16, 18, 19, 30, 34, 36, 38, 62, 58, 61, 62, 63, 83, 86, 88, 98, 100, 101, 112, 137

inspiration, inspire | 12, 14, 18, 19, 23, 28, 34, 51, 60, 64, 67, 69, 76, 77, 85, 86, 90, 91, 103, 112, 114, 115, 124, 137

S

service | 11, 12, 14, 16, 20, 23, 24, 27, 28, 30, 32, 35, 36, 39, 40, 44, 48, 60, 62, 64, 65, 68, 88, 89, 92s, 96, 102, 103, 109, 110, 117, 135
service based elevator pitch | 103
South Africa | 21
speaker, speaking | 11, 12, 15, 18, 19, 29, 32, 35, 37, 43, 46, 51, 56, 61, 83, 85, 103, 105, 106, 107, 112, 117, 122, 123, 137
subconscious | 124, 135
Synergetic Empathy™ | 23

T

thought leader | 12, 13, 29, 32, 61, 104, 106, 137
trust, truth | 14, 15, 26, 29, 30, 32, 33, 34, 36, 37, 44, 47, 50, 54, 60, 62, 66, 68, 81, 88, 96, 98, 99, 102, 110, 112, 117, 119, 135, 137

V

vision | 18, 23, 34, 35, 54, 67, 68, 69, 70, 74, 76, 81, 84, 85, 86, 119, 121, 122, 123, 126, 127, 128, 132, 133, 137

W

wealth | 27, 122, 126, 134
win-win | 14, 19, 23, 25, 34, 104, 136
wisdom | 25, 42, 65, 135
woo hoo! | (*"Because I finished my first book!"*)

PEOPLE

Marketing
With A Heart
A Principle Based Approach

PURPOSE   PROFIT